From Knowledge to Freedom

Bibliothèque et Archives nationales du Québec and Library and Archives Canada cataloguing in publication

Main entry under title:
Global Economy: The Foundation for the Next Era of Growth
Issued also in French under title: Économie mondiale : les fondements de la prochaine ère de croissance
Co-published by Décision média.
ISBN 978-2-89705-305-5 (Éditions La Presse)
ISBN 978-2-9811061-3-1 (Décision média)
1. Economic development. 2. International economic relations. I. Rémillard, Gil.
HD83.E2613 2014 338.9 C2014-941230-4

Publishers: Decision Media and Éditions La Presse
Edited by Gil Rémillard
Editor-in-Chief: Marie-Christine DuPont
Coordinator: Isabelle Boin-Serveau
Translation: Textualis
Cover page: Simon L'Archevêque
Typesetting: Guy Verville
Printing: Marquis Imprimeur

Éditions La Presse
Legal Deposit, second quarter 2014
ISBN 978-2-8970530-5-5

Decision Media:
ISBN 978-2-9811061-3-1

The opinions expressed in this book are those of the authors alone and do not necessarily represent the point of view of their organisation.

This book has been published in collaboration with the International Economic Forum of the Americas/Conference of Montreal

2075, University, suite 1701
Montreal, Quebec
H3A 2L1
Tel.: 514 871-2225
Fax.: 514 871-2226
montreal@forum-americas.org
forum-americas.org

THE
INTERNATIONAL
ECONOMIC FORUM
OF THE AMERICAS
20 years

GLOBAL ECONOMY

The Foundation for the Next Era of Growth

edited by
Gil Rémillard

CONTENTS

ACKNOWLEDGMENTS 7

FOREWORD

Gil Rémillard, Founding Chairman, International Economic Forum of the Americas, Professor, École nationale d'administration publique, and Counsel, Dentons Canada, LLP 9

PREFACE

Restoring Trust

Paul Desmarais, Jr., Chairman and Co-Chief Executive Officer, Power Corporation of Canada (PCC), Co-Chairman, Power Financial Corporation, president, Board of Governors, Conference of Montreal . . . 15

INTRODUCTION

Inclusive and Green Economic Growth

Angel Gurría, Secretary-General, Organisation for Economic Co-operation and Development. 19

GLOBAL ISSUES

For Sustainable Economic Recovery in Europe

Christian Noyer, Governor, Bank of France, and Chairman, Bank for International Settlements. 27

Immigration and Diversity as New Engines of Growth

Gordon Nixon, President and Chief Executive Officer, Royal Bank of Canada and Chair, Group Executive 34

Financing for African Economic Development

Donald Kaberuka, President, African Development Bank Group 42

The Global Trading System: Down but not Out

Perrin Beatty, President and Chief Executive Officer, Canadian Chamber of Commerce
Cam Vidler, Director, International Policy, Canadian Chamber of Commerce 50

GLOBAL ECONOMY

The Awakening of the Dragon
Pierre Lortie, Senior Business Advisor, Dentons Canada LLP 60

Sustainable Growth and Global Political Risks
Shaukat Aziz, Former Prime Minister of Pakistan and Former Executive Vice-President, Citibank. 71

Where Next for European Economic Integration?
Adam Steinhouse, International European Union consultant and affiliated professor, École nationale d'administration publique 80

ENERGY CHALLENGES

Energy Foundation for the Next Era of Growth
Maria van der Hoeven, Executive Director, International Energy Agency 89

Toward a Sustainable Energy Future
Christoph Frei, Secretary General, World Energy Council. 96

Natural Gas: A Winning Solution
Gérard Mestrallet, Chairman and Chief Executive Officer, GDF SUEZ 103

MANUFACTURING SECTORS

Manufacturing: A Promising Sector
Dominic Barton, Global Managing Director, McKinsey & Company 111

'Manufacturing the Future' With 3D
Avi Reichental, President and Chief Executive Officer, 3D Systems. 121

CONCLUSION

Five Factors of Growth Trends
Gil Rémillard 129

HISTORY AND MISSION

The Conference of Montreal 138

ACKNOWLEDGEMENTS

It all started when the Board of Governors, at its annual meeting last year (on June 10, 2013), decided that the 20th anniversary of the Conference of Montreal would be the perfect opportunity to publish a book on the world economy.

Marie-Christine DuPont, Editor-in-Chief of *Forces* magazine, agreed to take on the major challenge of coordinating this book, ensuring quality and maintaining deadlines.

We hardly know how to express our gratitude to her and her team.

- Alexandre Haarman
- Martin Dumas
- Caroline Jamet's staff Éditions La Presse

NICHOLAS RÉMILLARD
President and Chief Executive Officer,
International Economic Forum of the Americas

FOREWORD

The International Economic Forum of the Americas – Conference of Montreal was first held 20 years ago, in the wake of the economic globalization movement. This movement had been gaining momentum due to a number of factors: the creation of the World Trade Organization (WTO) (1995), the beginning of the economic and financial integration of the European Union through the Maastricht Treaty (1993), the signing of the North American Free Trade Agreement between the United States, Mexico and Canada (1994), and the beginning of the emergence of the BRIC countries (Brazil, Russia, India and China). In light of these developments, we sought to create an independent, international forum in Montreal that would foster a deeper understanding of the type of global economic system taking shape. Now, twenty years later, and six years after the Great Recession of 2008, where do we stand?

Although a number of uncertainties and challenges remain, the world economy seems well on its way toward a period of economic growth, propelled by a modest but firmly established American recovery. But what groundwork must be laid to ensure that this new era of prosperity is both sustainable and equitable? This is the broad theme chosen by the Board of Governors for the 20th edition of the International Economic Forum of the Americas – Conference of Montreal, to be held from June 9 to 12, 2014, with the goal of furthering the analysis of the various factors involved in the growth of the world economy in these critical times. The Board of Governors chose this theme at the recommendation of its Steering Committee, chaired by Hélène Desmarais. Each year, under her leadership, the Committee devotes considerable efforts to recommending the following year's theme to the Governors, for which I am grateful. It is certainly not an easy task, given the complexity, unpredictability and uncertainty involved in the global economy.

While no one predicted the economic crisis of 2008, it went down in history as the most serious and damaging financial and economic crisis since the Great Depression of the 1930s. The recession hit hard on a global scale, bringing us face to face with the failure of a system we believed was unshakable, based on the phenomenal growth of the emerging BRIC countries and the supposedly "Too Big to Fail" institutions. The bankruptcy of the Lehman Brothers in 2008 is a veritable spectre that still haunts us to this day. While we see a light at the end of the tunnel, we have the tendency to fear that, rather than being the distant glow of daylight, it's the headlight of a locomotive coming at us full steam.

Confidence still hasn't completely returned among consumers or investors. Economic indicators vary from one quarter to the next, resulting in expert analyses with widely divergent conclusions, while the value of currencies continues to fluctuate in relation to the U.S. dollar, which remains more than ever the world's dominant currency. Before stepping down as Chairman of the Federal Reserve, Ben Bernanke cautioned that what we needed to retain from the Great Recession of 2008 was to be wary of predictions. This is a wise message from a man who is credited with helping save us from the worst—but it is also a troubling one. It speaks to a scepticism which has many consequences, including the fact that companies have never had greater liquidity, yet are reluctant to invest, while consumers are dealing with their insecurity by saving their money.

There are more than economic concerns unsettling investment and consumer projects. We live in a time of profound change—social, cultural and political—which societies and their governments must come to terms with, caught as they are between the obligation to pay off their massive national debt on the one hand, and the need to support economic recovery on the other. This is a difficult balance to strike, as the International Monetary Fund (IMF) admitted when commenting on the situation in Greece.

We also need to make optimal use of the new communication, management and production methods that have been made available to us through the digital revolution. There is a veritable energy revolution underway, as we tap into more and more of the world's shale gas reserves and turn to alternative energy sources such as solar power. This has major repercussions on the economic and political world map—a map which is increasingly divided between self-sufficient countries and countries that are still dependent. But how long will this last? Indeed, the scene has been set for an industrial revolution, bringing to an end the economic divide between post-industrial countries and emerging ones. Also to be considered are the industrial consequences to the advent of 3D printing: dramatically reduced labour costs, guaranteed technological quality, and smaller production spaces. These are just a few of the major changes that are currently underway on a global scale, at a time where "fab labs" (fabrication laboratories)—innovative, digital-age workshops which meet new creative challenges and embody new values—are coming to the fore.

Boasting approximately 180 speakers, including some of the world's leading analysts and decision makers, the International Economic Forum of the Americas – Conference of Montreal, taking place from June 9 to 12, 2014, will once again provide insider knowledge to over 3,000 participants from across the globe.

Throughout its 20 years of existence, the Conference of Montreal has seen key moments that have resulted in a deeper understanding of global economic development. At the first edition of the conference in 1995, Paul Volcker, former Chairman of the Federal Reserve, stated that the problem of inflation among industrialized nations would be resolved through the globalization of economies, and ensuing competition laws. This man, who is credited with ending the record-high inflation of the 1970s, even went so far as to declare to a highly sceptical audience that it was, in fact, the dangers of deflation that should be of concern to us now. A mere three years later, Japan was hit with the problem of stagnation, and today, deflation is a major concern for many post-industrialized countries.

We also saw economist Jeffrey Sachs state in 1997 that the "Asian Tigers" would usher in the emergence of Asia, while a few hours later, economist and future Nobel-prize recipient Paul Krugman stated just the opposite, predicting a massive failure in the relatively short term due to a lack of internal capital and an over-reliance on foreign investors likely to turn tail and run at the slightest hint of danger. Six months after this declaration, globalization's first "speculative bubble" burst.

In 1998, Renato Ruggiero, then Director-General of the WTO, cautioned that bilateral and regional free trade agreements, which were then being signed all over the world, were in danger of killing the multilateral economic system of the WTO. The serious issues now facing the Doha Development Round, as well as the emergence of new transatlantic, transpacific and Asian commercial trade routes, perfectly illustrate his warning.

Participants of the June 2011 Conference will still remember the interview conducted by eminent American journalist Charlie Rose with General Pervez Musharraf, former President of Pakistan, who is currently under surveillance and facing the death sentence in his country. This was in the aftermath of the death of Osama bin Laden (May 2, 2011). General Musharraf warned us that the Taliban was more powerful than ever thanks to its strong presence in a number of regions in the world, particularly in Africa. History would prove him right.

Lastly, who could forget how Jean-Claude Trichet, who was at the time President of the Central European Bank, raised the alarm in June of 2007 regarding the dangers of elevated household debt. The rest is history, with the collapse of the housing bubble in fall of 2008.

The question is, are we any better equipped today to identify speculative bubbles? We are certainly more knowledgeable about the conditions under which they form and, more importantly, we have learned our lesson: a bubble, by its very nature, is bound to burst in the long run. The central banks must be particularly vigilant, as they are in front of the radar screen, as it were. But we must be vigilant as well, and avoid crying wolf unless we are sure there is indeed a danger. The central banks are well aware of this, and are doing remarkable work as they move into wholly uncharted territory. They have clearly understood that their main challenge today is instilling confidence in investors and consumers, who remain somewhat sceptical.

This book aims to present the different points of view on global economic systems in light of the next era of growth, which will be discussed during the 20th Conference of Montreal.

I would like to thank Paul Desmarais, Jr., Co-CEO of Power Corporation of Canada and Chair of the Board of Governors of the Conference of Montreal, for his tireless support since the start of the Conference, and for agreeing to write the preface to this book, which clearly details the problems arising from loss of confidence.

My sincere thanks also go to Angel Gurría, Secretary-General of the OECD, who makes a valuable contribution to the event year after year, and who has accepted the role of Conference Co-Chair for the 20th anniversary edition of the event. In his introduction to this book, Mr. Gurría provides a meaningful discussion of the challenges and uncertainties facing the world economy, while giving his perspective on a new global economic world order capable of ushering in an era of growth that is both sustainable and equitable.

I would also like to sincerely thank a great friend of the Conference, Gérard Mestrallet, Chairman and CEO of GDF SUEZ, for agreeing to co-chair this conference and for providing a comprehensive look at the various issues involved in the energy revolution.

Gil Rémillard

Founding Chairman, International Economic Forum of the Americas (IEFA), Professor, École nationale d'administration publique (ENAP), and Counsel, Dentons Canada, LLP

PREFACE

RESTORING TRUST

Welcome to *Global Economy – The Foundation for the Next Era of Growth,* a multi-authored examination of the current business state of affairs, compiled to mark the 20th anniversary of the Montreal Conference.

Churchill[1] famously said: "Now this is not the end. It is not even the beginning of the end. But it is, perhaps, the end of the beginning." That is where I believe we are now, at the end of the beginning. Five and a half years after the onset of the worst economic and financial crisis since the Great Depression, a great deal of reparation has been achieved, and it appears that the worst has been avoided.

There remains much work ahead of us, and as the aptly chosen theme for this 20th Montreal Conference urges, we must lay "the foundation for the next era of growth." There are budding signs of recovery, particularly in the world's largest economy, the United States. In the United Kingdom and in the United States, gradual withdrawal of monetary stimulus is in sight. There has been technological progress which increases the availability of affordable energy, particularly oil and gas, in North America. These factors combined suggest that we are poised to move on to the next phase, beyond *the beginning,* into "the next era of growth."

Given the challenges that still confront us, we can ill afford complacency. The recovery has been inconsistent, and unemployment remains at unacceptable levels in many quarters. Most countries

1 Speech at Mansion House, November 9, 1942. <https://www.winstonchurchill.org/learn/speeches/speeches-of-winston-churchill/1941-1945-war-leader/987-the-end-of-the-beginning>.

are still grappling with public deficits and debt at levels that leave future generations with worrying prospects. Emerging economies, long-time, major contributors to world growth, are now facing a less auspicious global environment and must adjust. Globalization, which has brought considerable benefits—in particular to consumers in the developed world and to workers in developing countries—is in need of a new impetus among growing geopolitical uncertainties.

I am convinced that one of the essential ingredients of success in meeting these challenges will be the restoration of trust.

Trust in the integrity of the markets, including the price signals, will enable consumers and producers to make the right decisions. Trust in the fairness of the economic system and of public policies will lead citizens to contribute their ingenuity, talents and skills to their nation's economy. Nations trusting each other in the context of a rapidly evolving world order will generate better global outcomes.

More truthful, more frequent communications are an essential element of creating and restoring trust. I truly believe that the Montreal Conference has played a significant role as a forum for such communications over the last 20 years. Therefore, I want to express my gratitude to the Governors of the Conference for their multi-faceted contributions to making the Conference into a well-attended and relevant event for global discussions.

Among the many high-caliber individuals who have been generous with their time and ideas over the years, I would like to give thanks to our two co-chairs of this year's Conference. Our co-chair and long-standing member of the Board of Governors, the highly respected Secretary-General of the Organisation for Economic Co-operation and Development (OECD), Angel Gurría, has contributed a chapter to this book. We are grateful to the OECD for partnering with the Montreal Conference for almost 20 years. The OECD, incidentally, is an excellent example of how leading research and its dissemination can improve trust among policy-makers and nations.

The other co-chair of this year's Conference, Gérard Mestrallet, Chairman and CEO of GDF SUEZ, is also a veteran member of the Board of Governors. He too has kindly agreed to write a chapter for this book, for which I wish to thank him.

Finally, I want to thank Christine Lagarde, Managing Director of the International Monetary Fund (IMF), for agreeing to become a member of the Montreal Conference's Board of Governors and for attending the Conference this year. The IMF provides noted leadership in research, coordination of policies and communications.

Restoring trust is a responsibility for everyone in a position of leadership and authority. The *end of the beginning* is the time to invest in this restoration of trust—among economic players, among citizens, among nations—to create a solid foundation for a new era of growth. Let us have informed and constructive discussions that will contribute to this essential global task.

PAUL DESMARAIS, Jr.

Paul Desmarais, Jr., Chairman and Co-Chief Executive Officer, Power Corporation of Canada (PCC), Co-Chairman, Power Financial Corporation, president, Board of Governors, Conference of Montreal

INTRODUCTION

ANGEL GURRÍA

Angel Gurría, Secretary-General of the Organisation for Economic Co-operation and Development (OECD) since June 2006. He was re-appointed to a second mandate in September 2010. As OECD Secretary-General, he has reinforced the OECD's role as a "hub" for global dialogue and debate on economic policy issues while pursuing internal modernisation and reform. Mr. Gurría is a Mexican national and came to the OECD following a distinguished career in public service in his country, including positions as Minister of Foreign Affairs and Minister of Finance and Public Credit in the 1990s.

INCLUSIVE AND GREEN ECONOMIC GROWTH[1]

Science has put the odds of humanity surviving the 21st century at 50/50[2]. The fundamental role of policymaking is to improve these odds. A resilient global economy is central to success, as is a shift in mind-set from economic to green and inclusive growth, ultimately focused on people's well-being. To achieve these goals, policymakers need to better understand interconnected challenges

1 The opinions expressed and arguments employed herein do not necessarily reflect the official views of the OECD's member countries.

2 Sir Martin Rees, UK Astronomer Royal, *Our Final Century*, Heinemann, 2003.

and find ways to shift the business-as-usual trajectory of the global economy.

Six years have passed since the beginning of the subprime financial crisis and our countries are still facing a bleak panorama. The crisis has left us with very heavy legacies. First of all, low growth: in 2013, GDP growth in OECD countries averaged 1.2% and we are expecting a meagre improvement to only 2.3% in 2014[3]. In the Euro area, we expect growth to reach only 1% in 2014 and 1.6% by 2015[4]. Secondly, high unemployment levels: there are over 200 million people unemployed in the world today, 62 million more than before the onset of the crisis[5]. Thirdly, growing inequality: inequalities in OECD countries grew more between 2007 and 2010—the worst years of the crisis—than in the preceding twelve years. Last but not least, an erosion of public trust in governments and institutions around the globe: according to the Gallup World Poll, trust in governments in OECD countries reached a record low of 40% in 2012 (down from 45% in 2007)[6].

With the space for fiscal and monetary tools practically exhausted, the OECD has been pointing to the only way forward, Going Structural. Structural reforms can boost growth, jobs and competitiveness, but they are also a most effective tool to build the foundations of the next era of growth. While designing and implementing structural reforms, it is also essential that we keep in mind the unique opportunity that we have to build a more resilient global economy powered by a more inclusive and more sustainable type of growth.

Inclusive Growth

The global economic crisis has reanimated a debate about the costs of 'growing unequal'[7]. In the wake of the financial crisis, vulnerable groups have disproportionally borne the brunt of adjustment in the labour market while the increased gap between rich and poor has led to intensive political and societal debate.

---

3 OECD. Economic Outlook, Nov. 2013.
4 *Idem*.
5 ILO. Global Employment Trends, 2014.
6 Gallup World Pol. Trust in Government, 2012.
7 OECD. Growing Unequal/Inclusive Growth Publication, 2013.

However, rising inequalities started well before the crisis, during periods of sustained economic growth. Inequality and exclusion affect people beyond income: better educated people live longer, health outcomes, educational opportunities and social mobility are disproportionately determined by socio-economic status.

Growing unequal thwarts opportunity and alienates individuals and vulnerable social groups from economic life. This, in turn, hampers society from using its human capital to the fullest potential, which stifles economic growth in the long term. There is therefore, a danger in growing unequal of unleashing a vicious circle, where rising inequalities, across a whole spectrum of outcomes that matter for people's well-being is accompanied by slow growth.

The next era of growth needs to work in favour of the many, not the lucky few. Recent OECD studies have confirmed that inequalities have been growing in the great majority of its member countries, reaching unacceptable limits. In the OECD, the average income of the richest 10% of the population is about nine and a half times that of the poorest 10%, up from seven times 25 years ago. In emerging economies like Mexico and Chile the difference is 27 to 1[8].

There is much that countries can do to tackle these inequalities. For example, policymakers can improve job opportunities through better education and skills; design innovative and effective policies to boost job creation; improve the tax and benefits system, the key tools to reduce inequality; and provide more efficient and accessible public services.

For this, it is necessary to foster more inclusive labour markets and enhance the employment prospects for all, but particularly for underrepresented groups, such as youth and older workers, people with disabilities and mental illness, women with young children, ethnic minorities and immigrants.

The OECD is working with a diversity of national policymakers to promote inclusive growth and restore the deeper foundations of economic resilience and human well-being. Inclusive growth requires a more integrated, multidimensional approach, with

8 OECD. Divided We Stand, 2011.

income and non-income outcomes considered. The framework considers the distributional effects of policies on different social groups, as opposed to a more conventional approach that focuses on the 'representative' or average individual or household. It is also essential to move beyond income and explore the areas that matter most for people's life satisfaction.

In this respect, the OECD Inclusive Growth Initiative *assists* policymakers in designing and implementing policies that foster synergies between pro-inclusiveness and growth-friendly policies; *mitigates* possible trade-offs; and *uses* inclusiveness as a driver of strong economic performance and growth.

A Green Growth

The unintended, and until recently unanticipated, consequences of the Great Moderation have also reanimated concerns about the environmental and ecological consequences of economic development. The debate of fostering green growth seems to have lost ground with the social impact of the crisis. As we tackle more extreme weather patterns with increasing frequency—forest fires, ice storms, floods and droughts, our awareness and concern over biodiversity losses has grown exponentially. And again, the impacts of environmental crises fall heaviest on the poor.

In building the economy of tomorrow, we have the opportunity—and the responsibility—to transit towards a type of growth that respects and nurtures the environment, what we call Green Growth at the OECD. The grave deterioration of the environment can no longer be ignored by our economic and financial policies.

We are on a collision course with nature! OECD analysis uses a "Baseline" scenario where unless the global energy mix changes, fossil fuels will supply about 85% of energy demand in 2050, implying a 50% increase in greenhouse gas (GHG) emissions and worsening urban air pollution. The number of premature deaths from exposure to particulate pollutants could double from current levels to 3.6 million every year. Global water demand is projected to increase by 55% to 2050. Competition for water would intensify, resulting in up to 2.3 billion more people living in severely water-stressed river basins. By 2050, global terrestrial biodiversity is projected to decline by a further 10%[9].

Continuing with the current production and consumption patterns and polluting energies—without taking into consideration the ecological health of our planet and our lives—is clearly not sustainable. The Intergovernmental Panel on Climate Change (IPCC) report, released in 2013, confirmed that warming of the climate system is unequivocal. In fact, since the 1950s, many of the observed changes are unprecedented over decades to millennia. The report also makes it clear that it is extremely likely that human influence has been the dominant cause of the observed warming since the mid-20th century.

Now the question is, how do we react? One major step in the right direction will be to effectively tackle CO_2 emissions, and here we confront a huge problem. Carbon dioxide is a long-lived gas—it hangs around. For every tonne of CO_2 emitted this year, some will still be around thousands of years from now. Even small ongoing emissions will continue to add to the atmospheric concentration. In other words, we have an accumulation problem. We are currently releasing over 30 billion tonnes of CO_2 annually. Of this, electricity and heat generation account for 41% and transport accounts for 22%[10]. Further anthropogenic emissions come from agriculture and the way we use land, together with some process emissions from industry.

For this reason, we should aim for the complete elimination of net emissions to the atmosphere from the combustion of fossil fuels. We can set our sights towards achieving this goal in the second half of the century. If we don't achieve this, we will condemn the coming generations to a very unpleasant existence.

To swim against the strong tides and effectively address the main policy challenges, our countries will need an Action Agenda focused on four key policy actions: putting a price on carbon; reforming fossil fuel subsidies; eliminating incoherent and inconsistent policies; and producing a new set of signals to consumers, to producers and investors.

---

9 OECD. Environmental Outlook to 2050.

10 IEA. Data for the year 2010. Source: IEA (2012), CO_2 Emissions from Fuel Combustion: Highlights.

In the implementation of Green Growth policies however, we need to be careful that they do not undermine each other. This can be done by examining the implications of one set of policies on the other i.e. enhance policy coherence. For instance:

- Phasing out or reducing environmentally harmful subsidies makes economic sense. By better targeting compensation measures for low-income households, or through separate social security systems, negative social effects can be avoided.
- Introducing or increasing environmental taxes or charges (e.g. energy taxes, water charges) to cover the full costs of resource provision and promote more efficient use, can have a negative impact on equity e.g. relatively higher costs for low income households. A full assessment of the distributional effects by income should include indirect effects, such as: price increases on taxed products; changes in employment opportunities associated with environmental taxes; and, consequent environmental gains/benefits.
- Green Growth policies, such as developing public transit and retrofitting energy efficiency in buildings, can contribute to more inclusive growth dynamics, particularly in urban areas[11]. However it is important to address trade-offs a priori. For example, the development of new eco-neighbourhoods can generate gentrification and result in the displacement of low income households[12]. To ensure that green growth contributes to social inclusion, energy efficiency policies in the building sector should also include social housing.

For a Better World

The largest crisis of our lifetimes has inflicted serious damage to our economies, our societies, and to our trust and expectations about the future. In a nutshell, the cost of this crisis has been historically high. However, it has also spread a positive and urgent need of change, it has confirmed that more of the same will be a big mistake, and it has opened a window of opportunity to revise our economic thinking and create the new set of ideas, policies

---

11 OECD. 2013.
12 Kamal-Chaoui and Plouin, 2012.

and values that we need to build more resilient, inclusive and sustainable economies.

This book is certainly a most effective provocation to renew our thinking, to push the horizon of knowledge and trespass conventional wisdom to build the next era of growth on a more solid and intelligent basis. I am sure that my fellow contributors to this book will challenge their own knowledge and imagination to foresee the new foundations of a better world.

GLOBAL ISSUES

CHRISTIAN NOYER

Christian Noyer, a former student of the École nationale d'administration, has been Governor of the Banque de France since 2003, and he is Chairman of the Bank for International Settlements (BIS). He is a member of the Governing Council of the European Central Bank (ECB) and Chairman of the Autorité de contrôle prudential et de résolution. Prior to that, he held various positions at the Treasury, including Director from 1993 to 1995, and served as the Chief of Staff for several Ministers of Finance. From 1998 to 2002, he was Vice-President of the ECB.

FOR SUSTAINABLE ECONOMIC RECOVERY IN EUROPE

The last few years have been rough for the Eurozone. First it was hit with the rest of the world by the financial crisis that was essentially imported from the United States. Then, it became the epicentre of a new period of tensions: the sovereign debt crisis. This economically violent series of events had major consequences for European growth. It also overturned certain essential foundations of the Eurozone, leading to a profound—and I believe beneficial—reassessment phase. All the parties involved—the governments, lacking rigour in managing their budgets prior to the crisis, the banks, at times careless, and the European institutions, often reacting too slowly or inadequately—have become aware of their responsibilities and attempted to draw lessons from the crisis, by implementing courageous reforms addressing all the causes which led to the crisis. Public finances have been brought in line, the banking system has been profoundly revitalized, structural reforms have been implemented to improve economic competitiveness, and economic governance in the Eurozone has been strengthened.

Where do we stand at the start of 2014? It is certainly too soon to declare that the crisis is now behind us. However, we can reasonably say that 2013 was a turning-point in the gradual "normalization" of the economic and financial environment in the Eurozone.

The second quarter of 2013 marked the end of a long period of six quarters of recession. While the numbers remain modest, they show a return to a positive trend: 0.3% growth in the second quarter of 2013, 0.1% in the third, and 0.3% in the fourth. It should also be noted that this positive trend was shared by the principal "peripheral" countries at the end of last year, notably with a return to economic growth for Italy and Spain. In financial terms as well, we've seen significant normalization: bond markets in the periphery continue to stabilize and have regained sustainable rate conditions, while fragmentation in the Eurozone has decreased, as demonstrated by a drop in excess liquidities and TARGET2 balances, for example.

As we in the Eurosystem predicted, recovery has been underway since the middle of last year. However, this recovery started at a very low point, and it is still weak, fragile and uneven. This raises a question at the centre of economic debates in the Eurozone today: How do we secure and strengthen European recovery? What measures are needed to ensure sustainable economic growth in Europe?

Budgetary Improvements to Restore Confidence

As we well know, the derailment of the Eurozone's public finances has been a significant factor contributing to the economic crisis and its severity since 2010. A lack of individual rigour in administering budgetary policy and failure to comply with the collective rules set out in the Maastricht Treaty meant that most of our countries had already-weakened structural balances when the crisis hit. This made them extremely vulnerable to an economic slowdown, with decreased tax revenue due to a decline in economic activity, increased expenditures resulting from the implementation of recovery plans and rising unemployment rates.

Obviously, the first response to the sovereign debt crisis was to make budget improvements on an individual and collective level. The Eurozone countries quickly grasped this, and began to reduce their budgetary deficits with determination and courage. These efforts bore fruit: public debt in the Eurozone dropped from 6.4% at the end of 2009 to 3.4% at the end of 2013. Collectively speaking, the economic pillar of the Economic and Monetary Union was greatly strengthened through the implementation of the "Six Pack" regulations at the end of 2011. These legislative measures enhanced budgetary discipline by making sanctions more automatic, monitoring national budgets more thoroughly and introducing new measures to monitor macroeconomic imbalances.

Concerns have often been expressed regarding the negative impact of these budgetary consolidation measures on European growth. I believe that this is not the central debate of the economic crisis, given that when it occurred, the main priority was to rebuild confidence and stability, which in turn required countries to regain fiscal credibility. Even today, restoring confidence depends on governments' ability to respect their commitment to balance public finances. Therefore, these efforts must be maintained, although obviously in such a way as to limit negative repercussions on consumption and growth, for example, by concentrating on reducing unproductive public expenditures.

Structural Reforms: Conditions of Future Growth

While balancing the budget is a necessary condition to ensuring a strong and durable recovery in Europe, as it fosters investor and consumer confidence, it is certainly not the sole condition. Above all, European growth is contingent on improved competitiveness within a globalized environment. In this area, the Eurozone is obviously not lacking in assets and is well equipped to face the challenges of the 21st century. With 370 million consumers and significant buying power, Europe remains the largest market in the world. It's also the most integrated region on an economic level, boasting highly qualified manpower and excellent infrastructures. However, Eurozone countries are often unable to fully exploit these advantages due to an inflexibility that has developed over time, during periods of prosperity. Today, the international environment is more demanding: new and powerful competitors have appeared, and comparative advantages are changing. Structural reform is the only solution.

In this field as well, the Eurozone has made considerable progress in recent years, particularly in the countries registering the biggest competitiveness gaps compared to the rest of the zone, and, consequently, were harder hit by the crisis than their neighbours. Cost competitiveness, as measured by unit labour costs, improved significantly. For example, from 2008 to 2012, the accumulated increase in unit labor cost of the three countries under bailout programs (Greece, Portugal and Ireland) was less than 12 percentage points behind the Eurozone average. Current account balances are also showing a strong correction. For these same three countries, balances calculated as a percentage of the GNP improved by more than 9 percentage points between 2008 and 2012, and several countries were able to turn major commercial balance deficits into surpluses.

This progress is the fruit of major reforms in key areas relating to competitiveness, such as the labour and goods markets, social services and pension plans. Obviously, the effects of these reforms will primarily be felt in the medium to long term. This, combined with the fact that they involve society's "losers," is why it is so difficult to obtain a political commitment on these issues. However, this state of affairs has not deterred European governments, which have grasped the urgency of these reforms and now have strong incentives on a collective level thanks to the monitoring of macroeconomic imbalances in Europe.

There is still much work to do in order to further liberalize our goods and services markets, increase the flexibility of our labour markets and strengthen margins for our businesses, thus allowing them to invest in innovative technologies. This is without a doubt the most powerful engine for ensuring a strong and sustainable recovery that will result in job creation in the Eurozone.

Financing Sound Recovery

As growth slowly returns, the issue of financing the recovery has become a vital one. For a number of years, credit in the Eurozone has been stagnating or dropping. This is explained in part by a low credit demand, which is understandable during an economic downturn. However, not surprisingly, issues with credit supply are coming into play, with the consolidation of balance sheets in the wake of the crisis and the changes being made in light of new legislation. When demand increases, these credit supply issues will play a much bigger role. Big businesses have sought alternative financing solutions: more than ever before, they are going directly to the market for financing through the issuing of shares. This is not an option for smaller companies.

In light of this, one of the key issues in my mind for European recovery is the need to ensure that appropriate financing is available to fund the activities of small and medium-sized businesses, which represent approximately 70% of salaried workers and 60% of the added value of the Eurozone. How do we ensure this financing? First, we need to be able to count on stable banks that are able to offer credit at attractive (but safe) rates. The monetary policy adopted by the Eurosystem in 2008 has provided valuable support at this level by making liquidity available to Eurozone banks at historically low rates and in unlimited quantities against a broader range of collateral since the start of the crisis. In recent years, banks have made considerable efforts to adapt to new prudential rules, which have been designed to limit negative impacts on economic financing. These efforts continue to bear fruit, and should allow banks to resume lending in the current economy under favourable conditions.

At the same time, it's essential to foster strong, dynamic financing without financial intermediaries, and not just for big businesses. The Banque de France is highly involved in this area. In 2013, we contributed to the work carried out by the Place de Paris. It was primarily aimed at ensuring financing for medium-sized businesses by facilitating their access to capital markets, whether for their short-term needs through treasury notes, or for their long-term needs through private placements, for which we drew up a charter. In fact, the Paris Marketplace, with the support of the Banque de France, has acquired a simple, financially-sound vehicle for securitizing credit claims, designed to facilitate the refinancing of commercial credit in the market and the Eurosystem, particularly for small and medium-sized businesses.

I am convinced that sustainable European growth can be financed only if we have both a banking system capable of financing the economy, and financing solutions without intermediaries.

A Banking Union for Stability and Growth

The fragmentation of the European banking system was yet another factor contributing to the severity of the Eurozone crisis, and today remains an impediment to a stronger recovery. This is because credit is considerably more complicated in countries whose banking systems suffered during the crisis, and because fragmentation breeds doubt as to the overall financial stability of the Eurozone, both private and public. We need to keep in mind the vicious cycle that emerged at the centre of the crisis between sovereign and bank risks.

Here, again, European leaders were quick to grasp the importance of finding a solution to this breach in the institutional structure of the Economic and Monetary Union, and quickly reached a consensus on the need to implement a banking union. The main objective of the banking union is to make sure that Eurozone banks are considered "Eurozone banks" and not "Irish," "German," or "Italian." In other words, the goal is to guarantee that credit conditions across Europe are not dependent on location but rather on the quality of the borrower.

To this end, the first step is to instate federal supervision of banks, to ensure that the same regulations and control methods are applied everywhere. A supranational supervisor is best placed to assess the risks inherent to cross-border activities, and thus to protect and encourage such activities, while remaining impartial to any national bias, which can foster a tendency toward "economic introversion" in times of crisis. A supranational body therefore has greater credibility and can increase stability and confidence in Europe. At the end of 2012, European heads of state approved the adoption of a Single Supervisory Mechanism, and we are in the process of actively preparing its implementation. As of November 2014, the main banks in the Eurozone will be supervised by a federalized system under the aegis of the ECB. Additionally, the entire European banking system, including countries outside the Eurozone, will be regulated by a "Single Rulebook" drawn up by the European Banking Authority.

In the meantime, we need to conduct an exhaustive analysis of the asset quality of the 128 banks that will be subject to single supervision, including a resistance test in a crisis scenario. This is an unprecedented exercise with a three-part objective: foster transparency with regard to the state of the European banking system, implement the necessary corrective measures, and, lastly, restore confidence. Without a doubt, this exercise is a challenging one, but I believe it is also an opportunity for European banks to demonstrate that they have strengthened their balance sheets, and are now stable, credible and up to the task of financing a sustainable recovery in the Eurozone. If the banking union wishes to achieve its objectives, the single supervision must be rounded out by a single resolution mechanism. Negotiations are still underway in this area, and it is vital that an agreement be reached as quickly as possible.

In conclusion, I believe that the measures allowing for a sustainable recovery of European growth have been clearly identified by all stakeholders: budgetary credibility, structural reforms strengthening growth potential and competitiveness, and an integrated, sound financial system, able to finance a stronger economy. On all these levels, the considerable efforts made by the Eurozone countries over the past few years have already borne fruit. They must be maintained to ensure that the Eurozone emerges from this crisis even stronger than before. In the words of one of fathers of European integration, Jean Monnet, "Europe will be forged in crises, and it will be the sum of the solutions adopted for those crises."

GORDON NIXON

Gordon Nixon is chief executive officer of Royal Bank of Canada (RBC). He is also a director of RBC and chair of its Group Executive. He began his career in 1979 at Dominion Securities in Toronto. In 1986, he transferred to Tokyo to assume responsibility for the firm's operations in Japan. Dominion Securities was acquired by Royal Bank of Canada in 1987 and Mr. Nixon returned to Toronto in 1989 as a managing director of Investment Banking. In 1995, he was appointed head of Global Investment Banking and in 1999 became chief executive officer of RBC Capital Markets and a member of Royal Bank's Executive Committee. He was appointed president of Royal Bank of Canada on April 1, 2001 and chief executive officer on August 1, 2001. In December 2013, Mr. Nixon announced his intention to retire effective August 1, 2014.

IMMIGRATION AND DIVERSITY AS NEW ENGINES OF GROWTH

According to recent United Nations statistics, 232 million international migrants—3% of the planet's population, more than the entire population of Brazil—were living abroad in 2013.

Human migration is of course nothing new. In fact, the story of humanity is a story of migration. The Americas are a prime example of this phenomenon. Wave after wave of humans fanned across our western hemisphere a dozen or more millennia ago, to be followed by European settlers and, ultimately, by individuals from around the globe.

There can be little doubt that immigration, taken as a whole, fuelled economic growth and activity in the Americas for several centuries. The effects of these migrations were not entirely without negative consequences—one need only think of the impact on indigenous peoples. Taken together this speaks to the importance of both where and how migration happens.

But How will Immigration Fit into the Next Era of Growth?

International migration is a key factor of globalization and a central—and occasionally vexing—issue on most national agendas. The recent vote in Switzerland rejecting EU freedom-of-movement provisions and the ongoing impasse in the United States regarding immigration reform are but two examples.

I think the Canadian example—and the experience of my own company, RBC—offer a positive way forward in terms of immigration, one that others may wish to learn from. Immigration has been a key economic driver for Canada from its inception and, thanks to a robust government policy framework and the active participation of many stakeholders including business, is likely to remain so in the years ahead.

There are of course many facets to a robust immigration regime. These include ensuring border and internal security, finding refuge for those fleeing civil strife, brain drain and gain issues and concerns around the impact on employment and a nation's culture and values.

In my view, any nation significantly reducing immigration rates would likely be making a mistake. Imposing high tariffs, as happened with the infamous Smoot-Hawley Act in the United States, proved a well-meaning but wrong-headed approach to dealing with the Great Depression of the 1930s.

Canada: a Proper Balance

My reference point is my own nation, Canada. We have a history of being able to integrate people into our country—and not at the cost of their unique identities. We are far from perfect when it comes to immigration, refugee policy and social and economic inclusion, but I do think that, directionally, we are on the right track, one that will benefit our country for decades to come.

Canada is a nation of 35 million people and on average we welcome approximately 250,000 permanent immigrants each year. On a percentage basis, this is one of the highest rates among all industrialized countries. While that sounds like a large number, it is important to note that without immigration Canada would actually experience an overall decline in population over time, as our birthrate is at less than replacement level. The same would be true in countries like Germany, Norway and Sweden, were it not for immigration.

The Canadian government's policy objective is to strike a proper balance in terms of categories of immigrants, while also seeking to better match labour market needs in terms of current and projected skill shortages. In 2013, for example, 63% of immigrants came under the heading of "Economic"; 26.1% "Family" (typically family reunification); and 10.9% "Humanitarian" (including refugees).

Thus, contrary to popular perception, immigrants to Canada today cover a broad spectrum in terms of education, economic status and career objectives. While some do enter into the realm of providing services, significant numbers also participate in high tech jobs like computer programming, the skilled trades and the health field. Others exercise their entrepreneurial talents, starting their own businesses.

In contrast to several decades ago, when the largest proportion of our immigrants emanated from Europe and the United States, in Canada today South Asia and China predominate, with smaller but increasing numbers also coming from Africa and Latin America. It is estimated that by 2031, 28% of all Canadians will have been born outside Canada (vs. 20.6% today) and while not all immigrants are visible minorities, the number of people belonging to visible minorities—non-white—will double to ten million from five.

Immigration: between Challenge and Opportunity

Welcoming a quarter of a million new residents annually obviously presents challenges in terms of economic and cultural orientation.

But it also presents Canada with great opportunity. Indeed, I would submit that Canada's increasingly diverse immigrant population provides competitive advantages and enhanced long-term growth prospects that far outweigh any up-front costs associated with the effort.

Estimates of those costs—defined as public services utilized in excess of taxes paid—vary widely. A conservative Canadian think tank, the Fraser Institute, figures the annual per person cost to be $5,400 (all dollars are in US); Economists Krishna Pendakur and Mohsen Javdani of Simon Fraser University, on the other hand, peg the number at $405. Whatever the correct number, what we do know is that the cost typically diminishes over a relatively short period of time as individuals move into the economic mainstream.

Immigrants can also spur high levels of innovation, a key component of a growing economy. A recent Conference Board of Canada study found that immigrants make up 35% of the individuals holding Canada's university research chairs—much higher than their 20% of the population.

And while many initially retain close economic ties with their home countries—Statistics Canada estimates that 30% of immigrants send money home during their first 2 to 4 years, with an average amount of $1,450 per year—fully 80% of recently arrived immigrants ultimately become Canadian citizens.

Remittances illustrate how immigration can often benefit both the country of origin and the receiving nation. According to a published World Bank estimate, remittances world-wide in 2012 totalled $515 billion, with approximately $400 billion destined for developing nations. The Inter-American Development Bank, in a separate study, found that Latin America and the Caribbean in 2011 received $59 billion in remittances-- more than the total of all foreign direct investment and development aid for the region.

These remittances often provide real economic benefit to families back in the country of origin, providing the seed capital to help lift the standard of living for entire families in countries like the Philippines, Mexico and India, to name just three of the largest recipients.

But remittances are just part of the story. Several recent studies assert that recent immigrants foster increased trade and economic activity between their country of origin and current residency. At the macro level, an exhaustive study of 180 partner-countries carried out by the Swedish Ministry of Foreign Affairs (published in the June 2010 edition of the Journal of Economic Integration) found that "Foreign-born people are uniquely qualified to stimulate trade between their present country of residency and where they were born" and found a direct, measurable correlation.

At the micro level, a 2013 Conference Board of Canada paper examined recent immigration in the province of Saskatchewan and concluded that "A 1% increase in the number of immigrants living in Saskatchewan is associated with increases of approximately $30 million in imported goods and $41 million in exported goods"—not insignificant for a province with just over one million residents.

As a business leader, it is my firm belief that newcomers to Canada bring skills, knowledge, and networks that can help a company reach out to economic giants like Brazil, China and India, as well as smaller nations.

The Canadian Choice: Inclusion

The reason for Canada's relative success in terms of welcoming immigrants into Canadian society may be that we try to ease people in, rather than force-fit them. Where some nations self-describe as a melting pot, Canadians tends to think in terms of a mosaic. As former Prime Minister Lester Pearson once put it, "The destiny of Canada is to unite, not divide; sharing in cooperation, not separation or conflict; respecting our past and welcoming our future".

In 1971 Canada became the first nation in the world to adopt an official policy of multiculturalism. Building on our history of three founding peoples, French, English and First Nations (Aboriginal), as well as two official languages, French and English, the intent is to foster an appreciation of cultural diversity and celebrate one's heritage, all within an inclusive Canadian context. Where some, including the United Nations in their published reports, tend to speak of "integration", we more typically reference "inclusion" as a policy goal. This is a subtle but important distinction, one that implies an acceptance of other cultures rather than a subsuming into the dominant culture

For example, the Canadian government maintains a Ministry of Heritage in addition to a Ministry of Immigration and Citizenship and actively promotes awareness and retention of diversity in a variety of ways, including education, support for community centers and funding for cultural festivals. One outgrowth of this policy is that in Canada the use of a hyphen to describe one's nationality—as in Indo-Canadian, Norwegian-Canadian or Chinese-Canadian—comes without stigma. In that sense, Canada practices a form of cultural pluralism, where smaller groups within the larger society maintain their unique cultural identities. Norms and practices are accepted by the wider community, and in fact are valued, as long as they are consistent with prevailing law and values.

Another outgrowth of this pluralistic approach is that the very community-based associations and cultural centers encouraged by this policy often themselves act as a valuable resource for newly arrived immigrants, helping them navigate unfamiliar processes and policies and assisting with language study and other issues.

There are also a variety of non-profit organizations whose mission is to assist newly arrived Canadians, including the Immigrant ACCESS Fund, Career Bridge and the Toronto Region Immigrant Employment Council, which I have chaired for many years. These often provide a vital networking path for immigrants, helping business better understand their skills and capabilities.

In that regard, the private sector must play a pivotal role. As the leader of a major Canadian financial institution, I know very well the critical skills and talents that new immigrants bring to our communities as employees and as clients. Indeed, most in the business community understand that if Canada is to maintain and improve its standard of living, we must continue to be the destination of choice for skilled immigrants—scientists, professionals and entrepreneurs- as well as those with skilled trades.

RBC has been actively recruiting newcomers and our workforce has become more diverse. Not only is this the right thing to do, it is the smart thing. In fact it is a business imperative. Many other

Canadian companies—and all of our major financial institutions—do the same.

Banking, like most commercial activities, comes down to relationships and trust. We are in the people-business. In that context, it is very important that our workforce reflect the community at large. It means embracing diversity in the broadest sense—not only hiring people of different ethnic, religious or national backgrounds, without regard to gender or sexual orientation, but also encouraging diversity of thought by building a culture of inclusiveness.

We find that hiring a wider spectrum of employees leads to greater opportunity for our business, not just in Canada but internationally. For example recent immigrants from China have not only helped us connect better with the Chinese-Canadian community—one million strong and growing—but have also helped us identify business opportunities internationally. The same can be said for our Indo-Canadian, Mexican-Canadian and Brazilian-Canadian employees, who have opened doors into their communities and to their countries of origin.

Who better to understand and empathize with the challenges new immigrants face than those who have themselves recently experienced it? With their help, we have tailored products to meet the specific needs of new immigrants, including a "Welcome to Canada" program and a special unsecured credit card program so that newcomers can establish creditworthiness more quickly. RBC has about 12 million clients in Canada and over the last two years, approximately 20% of our new clients are immigrants, a number we expect to grow.

Internationally this in-house expertise has proven a huge asset—indeed, a competitive advantage—to have people who understand the culture, the language and the ins- and outs- of doing business in various countries. It allows us better access to new and often rapidly growing markets, which is good not only for RBC and other financial institutions and businesses, but for the Canadian economy as a whole.

Over time our understanding of what it truly means to create a diverse and truly inclusive workplace has evolved and it continues to do so. For example, where we once looked more narrowly at whether or not we had diversity as reflected in the numbers of people at the table at important meetings or strategy sessions, today we pay equal attention to whether or not those individuals are given an opportunity to voice their ideas or point of view. This is what we mean by diversity of thought and we believe that this type of inclusiveness will invariably result in better ideas and business solutions, much as happened when greater numbers of women were included in the decision making process.

And RBC is by no means alone in these types of efforts. Again, this reflects the sense that only by harnessing the full potential of our people, including recent immigrants, can Canada have the kind of future we would wish.

While Canada has a history of success through immigration, today's environment presents new and different challenges and there is more to be done. Canadian employers too often fail to hire recent immigrants with both the skills and credentials, in terms of university degrees or technical certifications, to do the job. The result, according to the Conference Board of Canada, is that too many of our immigrants are under-employed. A 2012 RBC Economics Unit study found that if immigrants were to earn equal pay, including pay for the unfilled jobs they are capable of, personal income would increase by $31 billion. That amounts to over 2.1% of Canada's total GDP.

As we look to the 21st century for growth, I would assert that a prudent and well thought-out immigration policy and delivery system is a critical element for any economy. The scale and scope of immigration will of course differ to suit the individual needs of nations. But our experience in Canada, for a century or more, has been on balance a positive one, for business and for society as a whole. The increased diversity of our population has made us stronger players on the world economic stage and more inclusive and understanding at home.

DONALD KABERUKA

Donald Kaberuka is currently serving his second five-year term as President of the African Development Bank Group (AfDB). He was first elected in 2005, becoming the seventh president of the Bank Group since its establishment in 1963. Mr. Kaberuka, had a distinguished career in banking, international trade and development and government service A national of Rwanda, he was the country's Minister of Finance and Economic Planning between 1997 and 2005. During this period, he oversaw Rwanda's successful economic reconstruction after the end of the civil war there. He initiated and implemented major economic reforms and introduced new systems of structural, monetary and fiscal governance, laying special emphasis on the independence of Rwanda's central bank.

FINANCING FOR AFRICAN ECONOMIC DEVELOPMENT

Over the last decade, greater stability, sound macroeconomic policies, improved terms of trade and blossoming partnerships with emerging economies have widened the economic policy space of African policy makers. These have helped promote a healthy resilience to internal and external shocks and maintain enviable growth, and especially broadly good macroeconomic performance.

However, there is growing concern that the benefits have not been inclusive and equitably shared. Such growth has not been inclusive because it has not broadened access to sustainable socioeconomic opportunities for more people, countries and regions, while not protecting the vulnerable. Income inequality, poverty, lack of participation and opportunities in the economy, and unemployment, particularly for the youth, remain high.

Moreover, Africa has a major infrastructure deficit, which continues to add breaks on economic growth, reducing trade and international competitiveness and retarding poverty reduction. Africa's infrastructure deficit is indeed huge. Only about 20% of Sub-Saharan Africa population has access to electricity. At current investment trends, less than 40% of African countries would achieve universal access to electricity by 2050. Access to other infrastructure services, such as paved roads and water and sanitation, is also limited.

Innovative Sources of Development Finance in Africa

Transforming Africa's "inherited natural wealth into created wealth"

One of the opportunities to leapfrog economic development and improve the lives of African people relates to the prudent and effective exploitation and management of the continent's immense inherited natural resource wealth. Africa has witnessed a boom in oil, gas and mineral resources discoveries in recent years. It has been estimated that Africa has in excess of 122 billion barrels of proven oil reserves (slightly more than this in potential reserves) about half those of Saudi Arabia, the world's largest producing-country. Deposits of natural gas are equally plentiful, estimated at about 500 trillion cubic feet of proven reserves, and the equivalent in potential reserves. In net present value terms, the potential revenue stream from this natural wealth is more than USD 605 billion per year. That is a third of Africa's GDP. Africa is also endowed with vast amounts of non-oil mineral resources. Globally, it produces 82% of platinum, 24% of phosphate, 25% of titanium, 18% of uranium, and 5% of nickel. "Rare earths" are thought to be plentiful in some parts of Africa. World prices for all these metals have increased dramatically during the 2000s.

If harnessed carefully natural resources could provide a good basis for rapid, sustained and inclusive development. It will involve translating these inherited natural resources into created wealth.

A tax regime that raises revenue without discouraging private sector participation should also be encouraged. It is important to negotiate fair deals from the start. African governments receive only about 12% of the royalties on oil and/gas production compared to Latin America's 24%.

It is vital to reduce corruption, negotiate more beneficial and transparent contracts with oil companies, and ensure that natural resource companies do not evade taxes. Resources must also be distributed more equitably among the population, taking into account the local socio-political and ethnic context, while revenues should be directed into investments in other sectors to diversify the economy. Checks and balances need to be maximized through parliament.

Resource-backed financing is another important source of financing in the Continent. These are loans for development backed by natural resources. For example, Chinese investments in Angola, Nigeria, and Sudan are backed by oil, in Gabon by iron, in Ghana by cocoa, and in the Democratic Republic of the Congo by copper. It is critical that African governments negotiate equitable deals that correctly value the resources assigned and environmental externalities. The share of royalties and dividends should also be robust to fluctuations in world commodity prices. This form of financing can be re-configured for local investors.

African countries can also tap carbon finance markets to finance low-carbon development projects such as those in infrastructure. So far though, access to carbon credits by clean technology projects in emerging markets and developing countries has had mixed results across regions, with Africa lagging substantially behind.

Commodity-linked debt instruments present another useful development financing source. In August 2010, for example, South Africa's Standard Bank Group offered Rand-denominated notes traded on the Johannesburg Stock Exchange whose returns were linked to the performance of precious metals. The capital was protected and the notes had specific redemption dates. Commodity exporters across Africa could potentially use such instruments to raise funds and hedge against commodity price fluctuations.

Innovative Government Financing Instruments

Bringing the Informal Sector into the Tax Net

As ODA declines and FDI becomes increasingly volatile and concentrated, taxation will become even more important for the provision of services and public investments generally.

Government infrastructure bonds

These are government bonds issued on the domestic market to finance public infrastructure projects.

Private sector Local currency infrastructure bonds

The issuance of public local infrastructure bonds has paved the way for corporate bonds issues by the private or state-owned companies.

Innovative Private Financing Instruments

Private equity funds

These funds mobilize financing primarily from both international and local institutional investors and traditional financiers, such as Development Finance Institutions.

Corporate bonds

These are domestic bonds issued by private firms. South Africa's private sector has been able to tap local capital markets to finance infrastructure projects in water, transportation, and power. The country's capital markets are well developed and long-term credit is available, as well as expertise to arrange more complex transactions such as the EUR 2.5 billion Gautrain project.

Mobilizing other domestic resources

African governments should also mobilize other domestic resources. Removing exemptions and strengthening tax administration would increase public tax revenues. In African countries, where large informal sectors impede effective direct taxation, excises, value-added taxes, and other indirect taxes can be relied upon.

Incentivizing Private investment

African governments have a critical role to play in providing incentives for private investment in development projects. Such incentives could include risk mitigation instruments, such as viability gap financing, among others.

Public-Private Partnerships

Another funding source is the use of public-private partnerships (PPPs). It is imperative that companies in the private sector have to be largely involved in African development through PPPs, especially in infrastructure development.

Specialized infrastructure funds

These are funds created by established infrastructure firms, including upstream industries, which invest in various infrastructure projects.

Tackling sector-specific inefficiencies

Governments need to provide incentives to reduce market inefficiencies of specific sectors. In playing its role as financier, the public sector should seek to improve efficiency in the delivery of development finance.

The Role of Sovereign Wealth Funds (SWFs)—Local and Foreign

When well designed and implemented, SWFs can be a significant source of finance for both domestic and foreign projects. The global Sovereign Wealth Funds (SWFs) currently control an aggregate of approximately US$6.00trillion in assets under management (AUM). Based on historical databases on SWFs' transactions, SWFs, especially those from African and Arab countries, can facilitate up to 50% of the investment needs in infrastructure in Africa over the 2010-20 decade. From an investment perspective, Africa's infrastructure projects for SWFs are attractive for different reasons: higher historical returns compared to other asset classes (bonds, equities, real estate), low correlation with traditional asset classes, the long-term nature of the investment is in line with the mandate of most sovereign wealth funds, revenues are implicitly linked to inflation, and cash flows are reasonably stable and have a low elasticity of demand. The SWF amount may be significant and may leverage other funding; and Africa needs long term and stable funding, that SWFs can bring.

When investing in Africa, SWFs can engage in increased co-operation with the AfDB, especially in the context of the recently launched Africa50 Fund. While African countries designing and establishing the missing investment products and services (i.e. tenor extension, first loss guarantees, credit enhancement, exit options, etc.) as well as ring-fencing the prospects for healthy returns, improving the enabling environment, and sustained reform efforts, an innovative vehicles such as the Africa50 Fund is a welcome and important support.

In addition, the recently established initiatives in support of risk mitigation for investments relevant for Africa's infrastructure include the Initiative for Risk Mitigation in Africa (IRMA), which is housed at the AfDB. IRMA provides a brokerage service for private investors and African governments who need risk mitigation coverage. It also acts as a platform for disseminating information on available risk mitigation instruments for infrastructure projects in Africa.

Unlocking Value from Foreign Financing

While *diaspora bonds* are government bonds targeted at a country's diaspora, they can also be offered to the local population. Ethiopia pioneered diaspora bonds with its *Millennium Corporate Bond* in 2007. The bond raised capital for the state-owned Ethiopian Electric Power Corporation. Other sub-Saharan African countries with large diaspora could raise up to US$5 billion to US$10 billion per year through the issuance of such bonds.

There are opportunities to unlock significant additional value from international remittance flows through the expanded use of diaspora bonds. This could be assisted by customizing the regulatory framework for the creation and sale of bonds in foreign countries at the international level since this lower the costs of compliance across multiple jurisdictions and speed up the regulatory-approval process. In addition, donor-country governments should commit to sharing reliable demographic data with their African counterparts to facilitate the marketing of bonds to diaspora. The G20 should also implement its commitment to cut the global average cost of these transactions down to 5 percent.

Securitizing remittances also allows countries with fairly predictable remittance flows to borrow on international markets on the back of expected future remittance flows.

Transforming Foreign Direct Investment

Measures are needed to transform and capture the full value of FDI in Africa.

Tracking and Stopping Illicit Financial Flows

In addition to mobilizing other external resources outside of ODA, tackling illicit financial flows from Africa should be at the center of resource mobilization to finance Africa's development.

The Role of the African Development Bank Group

The African Development Bank's Ten-Year Strategy for 2013–2022, which reflects the aspirations of the entire African continent, is designed to place the Bank at the center of Africa's transformation and to improve the quality of Africa's growth. The Strategy is built around two objectives, notably, to improve the quality of Africa's growth: inclusive growth, and the transition to green growth. The overarching objective of achieving growth that is more inclusive will lead not just to equality of treatment and opportunity but also to deep reductions in poverty and a correspondingly large increase in jobs. It will also lead to the expansion of the economic base across the barriers of age, gender and geography. In addition, the Strategy is meant to help Africa gradually transition to "green growth" that will protect livelihoods, improve water, energy and food security, promote the sustainable use of natural resources and spur innovation, job creation and economic development. These two objectives are supported by five operational priorities in which the Bank has unmatched advantage, expertise, access and trust. These operational priority areas include infrastructure development, regional economic integration, private sector development, governance and accountability, and skills and technology. In addition, in implementing the ten-year Strategy, the Bank will pay particular attention to fragile states, agriculture and food security, and gender.

Given the lean resources at its disposal, the Bank is seeking new and creative ways of mobilizing resources to support Africa's transformation, especially by leveraging its own resources. The Bank will explore options for attracting additional investment from emerging economies and from new funders and donors, including sovereign wealth and pension funds.

The Bank has introduced the use of quasi-equity instruments, such as subordinated loans, to raise the overall return on investment, and/or to enhance credit structures to acceptable risk levels. To address exchange rate risk, the Bank has developed the innovative Currency Exchange Fund. The Fund helps investors hedge against interest rate risks associated with infrastructure financing in local currencies. The Bank has also become increasingly more involved in issuing bonds in local currencies, providing guarantees, and participating in currency swaps markets. In addition, it is promoting capacity building in RMCs to build efficient and sustainable institutions and regulatory frameworks that are robust enough to develop even the most complex projects.

The AfDB is championing a new initiative—Africa50 Fund—to be deployed to finance only transformational projects deemed a priority and show a good return. The Africa50 Fund was endorsed by African Finance Ministers at the Bank's Annual Meeting in Marrakech in May 2013.

Conclusion

For a long time development financing in Africa was largely dependent on external sources. Of late, however, several countries are making important sorties into the capital markets. Domestic resource mobilization for that purpose is on the increase. Increasingly, where policy reforms have clarity and predictability, private investors are able to turn these obstacles into opportunities. However, the development financing gap seems daunting. So now is the time to think out of the box, time for a step change. Fifty years after independence, it is time for that step change. The step change involves Africa taking ownership, mobilizing its own energies and resources, putting those savings to build Africa's infrastructure and in the process getting a good return. That is the genesis of Africa50 Fund I mentioned above.

PERRIN BEATTY

The Honorable Perrin Beatty is President and Chief Executive Officer of the Canadian Chamber of Commerce, which represents over 200,000 businesses. He started his career in politics, where he held a number of cabinet portfolios, including External Affairs and Defense. Afterwards, he was President of the CBC and President and Chief Executive Officer of the Canadian Manufacturers & Exporters. He is Chancellor of the Ontario Institute of Technology (OIT) and President of the B20 Coalition.

CAM VIDLER

Cam Vidler is Director of International Policy at the Canadian Chamber of Commerce. He has a background in trade, investment and development policy, having previously worked for the Canada-India Business Council, UNCTAD, World Bank and Fraser Institute. Cam has a BA (hons) from the University of Toronto and a Masters degree in international affairs from The Graduate Institute of International and Development Studies in Geneva, Switzerland.

THE GLOBAL TRADING SYSTEM: DOWN BUT NOT OUT

The history of the Conference de Montreal is closely tied to the history of globalization and the international trading system. Founded in 1994—the year that the World Trade Organization (WTO) was created and the North American Free Trade Agreement (NAFTA) entered into force—the Conference has for two decades brought together leaders from government, business and civil society around the world to develop a better understanding of opportunities and challenges that come with rising economic integration.

The global economy has evolved considerably since the early years of the Conference. During its first decade, the world witnessed spread of open markets for goods, services and capital. Cross-border trade and investment flourished, and previously closed economies took advantage of unprecedented growth opportunities. Integration slowed somewhat during the Asian financial crisis in the late 1990s, and then picked up at an even greater speed as the world entered the new millennium.

But the trading system was about to face a series of tests. Persistent macroeconomic imbalances, the financial crisis and subsequent recession, and the rise of the BRICs all shook the system's geopolitical and institutional foundations. The Doha Round of WTO negotiations stalled, leaving key issues including services, investment and agriculture stranded on the table. There has been a resurgence in protectionism since the crisis six years ago. International trade and investment flows have yet to recover.

Thankfully, the mood appears to be shifting. The WTO Ministerial Conference in Bali in 2013 yielded an agreement on trade facilitation. Although it covers just a portion of the initial negotiating agenda at Doha, it is nonetheless the first multilateral trade agreement in over two decades. There are other multilateral talks on services and environmental goods. At the same time, the world's leading trading powers have launched major regional and bilateral negotiations. It is hard to say at this stage if these recent events will amount to a real strengthening of the trading system, but there are good reasons to be optimistic.

Trade as a Force for Good

The future of free trade is important to all of us. The theory is elegant: by allowing countries and regions to specialize in what they do best, and by exposing firms and workers to international competition, trade maximizes economic efficiency and translates into higher productivity and incomes across the board. Theory and practice can differ, however, and as the pernicious effects of the Great Recession persist, this vision is increasingly under attack. Voices as diverse as Occupy Wall Street and Pope Francis blame the globalized economy for rising inequality and stubborn unemployment.

So what has the record been? A recent paper by World Bank economist Branko Milanovic that looks at global income distribution from 1988 to 2008 tries to answer this question.[1] He found that while the top one percent of the population made significant gains, the middle classes of emerging markets—hundreds of millions of people living in China, India, Brazil, Indonesia and Egypt, among others—saw their incomes rise at an even faster rate. Such an exceptional feat of poverty alleviation would never have been possible without access to affluent markets and injections of foreign capital and technology.

The political benefits of trade are no less important. Domestically, trade openness fosters a dynamic private sector that does not rely on the government of the day to protect it from competition. This independence is a necessary—though not sufficient—condition for the development of vibrant civil societies that can hold governments to account. It is the path taken by countries like South Korea, Chile and, some might even say, China.

Since Immanuel Kant, it has been argued that international trade helps prevent conflict. When a country comes to expect another to buy its products or to supply it with essential goods and services, its government has an incentive to avoid actions that would harm or halt these flows. Of course, while economic interdependence creates encourages peaceful collaboration, it cannot guarantee it. The European economies were highly integrated at the dawn of World War I. But during the second half of the 20th century, trade formed the basis of the European project, which has made war far less likely among countries where millions of people died in conflicts that tore the continent apart just a generation or two before.

Today, the pacifying effects of trade are perhaps most visible and most important in East Asia. While tensions between Japan and

---

1 Milanovic, Branko. 2012. "Global Income Inequality by the Numbers: in History and Now." Policy Research Working Paper Series No. 6259. The World Bank. p. 13.

China over the Senkaku islands and other bilateral issues are running high, both countries have a powerful incentive to manage their disputes peacefully. China continues to be Japan's largest customer: exports expanded at an annual rate of 18% in late 2013. Japan is the fifth-largest market for Chinese businesses.[2] Two-way tourism is booming. Former Canadian Ambassador Joseph Caron put it well when he recently wrote: "Whether their current leaders like it or not, China, Korea and Japan are now mutually dependent. And it is generally better to like it."[3]

System under Threat: the Paradox of Globalization

Free trade does not materialize on its own. It depends on strong political and institutional underpinnings. For political leaders to open their domestic markets and face potentially fierce opposition from previously protected industries, they need credible assurances that others will do the same. They also need to believe that once these markets are open, principles of fair competition will apply. Subsidies, regulatory barriers or other forms of targeted support that give firms from one nation an advantage over those from another can erode the will to trade.

After World War II, the U.S. and its allies put the conditions in place for trade to flourish. Making up the vast majority of world output, these countries committed to open their markets and created the General Agreement on Trade and Tariffs (GATT) which eventually became the WTO to guide further liberalization and settle disputes. A robust body of international trade law developed. The International Monetary Fund was established to help countries with balance of payment pressures finance their current account deficits, thereby removing the need for them to block imports.

With these institutions in place, tariffs were reduced across the world and markets were opened up to foreign capital. Trade and investment grew exponentially. Developing countries were pulled into global production networks, and a number of them became trading powers in their own right.

---

2 Ivanovitch, Michael. December 29, 2013. "China and Japan trading goods and war threats." <http://www.cnbc.com/id/101300548>.

3 Caron, Joseph. January 30, 2014. "The Abe Dilemmas." *Canada-Asia Agenda*. Asia Pacific Foundation of Canada: Vancouver.

In an interesting twist, however, the trade-fuelled rise of China and other new players put pressure on the post-War system of global economic governance. This view is best captured by Ian Bremmer's concept of a G-Zero world.[4] He argues that the crisis and recession sapped the capacity and consent of North America, Europe and Japan to lead on international economic affairs. New to the scene and faced with their own domestic challenges, the BRICs have been either unable or unwilling to fill the gap.

The alternative—consensus governance through broader groups such as the G20—is proving difficult because of profound differences in economic models. The BRICs' embrace of markets has been cautious. Their governments have been happy to take advantage of the export opportunities brought about by the growth of international trade, but somewhat less agreement to open up at home. And the commanding heights of the economy remain firmly under state control: the majority of the largest companies in these countries are owned by the government.[5] This raises concerns about fair competition.

In this context, it's perhaps not a surprise that we have seen an increase in protectionism among both the advanced and emerging economies since the recent recession. According to Global Trade Alert, the number of protectionist measures implemented around the world since 2008 has exceeded the number of liberalizing measures by a factor of three.[6] This is despite a rolling pledge by the G20 to champion unencumbered commerce. Until recently, the Doha Round was lifeless and despite the steady growth of bilateral or regional trade agreements, they tended not to cover the world's most important trading relationships. Today, trade as a share of world GDP is barely at its pre-crisis level, and foreign investment figures have fared even worse.[7]

---

4 Bremmer, Ian. May 14, 2012. "Welcome to the New World Disorder". *Foreign Policy.*

5 Kowalski, Przemyslaw; Büge, Max; Sztajerowska, Monika and Matias Egeland. 2013. "State-Owned Enterprises: Trade Effects and Policy Implications." OECD Trade Policy Paper No. 147. p. 23.

6 Evenett, Simon J. 2013. "What Restraint? Five years of G20 Pledges on Trade: The 14th Global Trade Alert Report." Centre for Economic Policy Research, London.

7 *The Economist*. October 12, 2013. "The gated globe." <http://www.economist.com/news/special-report/21587384-forward-march-globalisation-has-paused-financial-crisis-giving-way.>

The post-crisis years have not been kind to international trade and the institutions that support it. Indeed, global governance across a wide range of has suffered. But things are not as bad as they seem.

First off, the volume of trade recovered much faster than it did during the Great Depression, where a steady decline lasted nearly a decade.[8] And although there was a brief spike in the use of anti-dumping duties to protect domestic industries, by 2011, the number of cases had dropped to their lowest level since the founding of the WTO.

Trade liberalization efforts have also gathered steam. The most notable is the WTO agreement announced in Bali. At its core is an agreement on trade facilitation, which will require countries to reduce red tape and improve transparency in their customs administration—making it easier for importers and exporters to move their goods across borders. Fully implemented, it could lower global trade costs by up to ten percent.[9]

The symbolic benefits of the Bali package are perhaps even greater. Had the Ministerial failed to produce an outcome, it could have permanently undermined the WTO as a platform for further trade liberalization. The agreement instead gave the organization and its member states a chance to rethink their approach to the rest of the Doha Round. An intensive work program is underway to develop a new action plan for the negotiations, whether that means replicating the Bali approach and breaking up remaining issues into digestible morsels, or adding new issues to give negotiators more bargaining chips.

At the World Economic Forum in January 2014, China, Japan, the United States, the European Union and a number of other advanced and emerging economies—covering eighty-six percent of global trade—announced that they would pursue an agreement to liberalize trade in environmental goods. This initiative will take place under the auspices of the WTO, allowing others to accede to the agreement after it is completed.

---

8 Drezner, Daniel. October, 2012. "The Irony of Global Economic Governance: The System Worked." Working Paper. New York Council on Foreign Relations.

9 Moïsé, Evdokia, Thomas Orliac and Peter Minor. 2011. "Trade Facilitation Indicators: The Impact on Trade Costs." OECD trade Policy working Paper no. 118. Paris: Organization for Economic Cooperation and Development.

A similar approach is being taken to barriers to trade in services, an increasingly important sector where liberalization efforts have lagged. Launched in 2012 by the OECD countries as a response to the lack of progress in the Doha Round, talks towards an international Trade in Services Agreement now include over twenty participants covering over seventy percent of world's trade in the sector. China formally asked to join last fall.

Then there are the so-called 'mega-regionals', including the twelve-country Trans-Pacific Partnership (TPP), the European Union's bilateral talks with the United States and Japan, the Pacific Alliance between Mexico, Colombia, Peru and Chile, and the Regional Comprehensive Economic Partnership (RCEP), which covers China, Japan, India, South Korea, ASEAN, Australia and New Zealand. China, Japan and South Korea are also negotiating their own trilateral deal.

Preferential agreements, whether bilateral or regional in nature, have often been viewed with suspicion by advocates of a common global trading system. This is because they only open certain markets to certain countries, and their strict rules of origin can impede the development of multinational supply chains that fragment production across a wide range of countries to take advantage of unique competitive advantages.

But today's mega-regionals are different. To start with, they are more inclusive. Take the TPP: its ambition is not to create a closed-off trading block that gives advantages to insiders at the cost of outsiders, but to develop new common rules on "21st Century" trade issues—like regulatory cooperation, state-owned enterprises and the digital economy—that can serve as a template for future agreements. Sometimes framed as a U.S.-led initiative, the TPP is open to other major trading countries. Canada and Mexico joined in 2012, Japan joined last year, and South Korea may be right behind them. Even China has changed its stance from open hostility to cautious interest.

Initiatives like the TPP need not weaken the multilateral system. Progress here may in fact cause those left out to work harder at the WTO to keep up, just as NAFTA arguably helped drive the conclusion of the Uruguay Round in the early 1990s. The proliferation of regional deals gives the WTO the opportunity to take on new functions. The organization is well-placed to help ensure the consistency of provisions and rules across different regional agreements, and to identify which of these should be brought up to the multilateral level.[10]

There is also the potential to knit together regional deals through incremental adjustments to rules of origin. Canada, Colombia and Peru are doing just that to ensure that the three bilateral agreements they share can be used to their full potential. Businesses operating under different agreements are increasingly pressing governments to integrate or streamline them in order to ensure the smooth operation of their supply chains.

It is too early to tell whether this flurry of activity amounts to a real turning point. Most of the negotiations have yet to be concluded, and some of them are starting to drag on. Those that come to fruition may be superficial, with exclusions for sensitive sectors and space for governments to subvert the spirit of free trade through other means. Nonetheless, the global trading system is in a better place than it was, and remains stronger than many of its critics suggest.

Reasons for Optimism

So what explains the resilience of the global trading system in face of geopolitical trends that indicate otherwise?

To start with, the relative decline of United States and its traditional allies has been exaggerated. Growth rates in leading emerging markets have fallen sharply, while recovery is starting to take hold in North America and Europe. In Japan, the Abe government has taken significant measures to unlock long-term growth. A renewed willingness of these countries to open their markets is what underpins today's regional and bilateral trade talks. The U.S. was instrumental during the Bali Ministerial, single-handedly reaching a compromise with India that allowed the trade facilitation package to be announced.

For the first time, the U.S., EU and Japan are negotiating trade agreements among themselves. Aligning or harmonizing standards and regulations would create further opportunities for exert

10 Baldwin, Richard. January 20, 2014. "Multilateralising 21st century regionalism." VoxEU.org. <http://www.voxeu.org/article/multilateralising-21st-century-regionalism>.

collective leadership. The big test, however, will be whether U.S. Congress is willing to provide the current or a future President with 'fast-track' authority. Failure on this front could signal a waning appetite in the U.S. to take the lead on trade.

The evolution of business interests is another factor. Put simply, years of relatively open trade have strengthened companies and lobby groups that are outward-oriented at the expense of those that see trade as a threat.[11] This was apparent in the almost universal push to conclude the Bali package by groups such as the International Chamber of Commerce, World Economic Forum, Business and Industry Advisory Council (BIAC) to the OECD and B20. These groups worked tirelessly in capitals around the world to convey the benefits of an agreement on trade facilitation and the dangers of failing to produce one.

Desperation also has something to do with it. Trade policy is one of few tools left to jumpstart growth. The financial crisis and subsequent recession have largely exhausted the monetary and fiscal firepower of governments. The U.S. Federal Reserve is reducing its asset purchases, and the European debt crisis forced many countries there to raise taxes and reduce spending. China and other emerging markets are reigning in excess liquidity to counter the risks of inflation or property bubbles. Even Canada, which fared relatively well through the recession, is now focused on balancing the books. With the global recovery underway but still lackluster, politicians around the world are looking to trade liberalization as a low-cost strategy to boost output and employment. Trade figured prominently in the G20 Finance Minister's recent announcement of a joint plan to boost global growth by $2 trillion.

Ideas matter too. One needs to look no further than the OECD and WTO's work on global value chains. The core message is that, in today's globalized economy, the competitiveness of exports depends on how easily imports can enter your market. New statistics have revealed the scale of countries' interdependence and the harm that results from import tariffs and poor customs and admin-

---

11 Baldwin, Richard and Frédéric Robert-Nicoud. 2008. "A simple model of the juggernaut effect of trade liberalisation." Centre for Economic Performance, London School of Economics and Political Science, London, UK.

istrative procedures. This research added intellectual weight to the trade facilitation agenda pushed by the global business community in the run-up to Bali.

The world economy and how it is governed have changed dramatically since the first gathering of the Conference de Montreal, when the global spread of free markets seemed almost inevitable. The rapid and somewhat unexpected rise of emerging economies that followed significantly altered the balance of power and diversity of economic models. For a few years at least, it seemed that this transformation could erode the international cooperation needed to backstop the global trading system.

Fortunately, recent progress at the multilateral and regional level suggests a positive outlook. Several factors are responsible: renewed leadership from the U.S., Europe and Japan, an increasingly united global business community, the exhaustion of other policy options to stimulate growth, and a more sophisticated understanding of global supply chains. Assuming these factors are strong enough, the 20th anniversary of the Conference may mark the beginning of a new wave of liberalization, just as its founding did in 1994.

PIERRE LORTIE

Pierre Lortie, M.C., FCAE is a Senior Business Advisor at Dentons Canada LLP, a major Canadian law firm recognized as a leader in business related legal matters across Canada. He is President of the Canadian Academy of Engineering, and, among other, Director of the Research Center of the McGill University Health Center and Director and member of the Executive Committee of the Conference of Defence Associations Institute. He has recently served as a member of the Asia Pacific Foundation Taskforce on Canada's strategies towards the regional institutional architecture that governs in Asia.

THE AWAKENING OF THE DRAGON

For over two centuries the West has dominated the world. At the dawn of the 21st Century, we are witness to an historic realignment where the nations of Asia, home to over half of the world's population, are playing an increasing leading role. Today, three Asian countries are amongst the ten largest national economies. The ascendency of Asia reflects the unprecedented levels of economic growth experienced by China and India—two very populous and continental-sized states—and highlights the dynamism underlying the resurgence of Asia on the global scene. Consonant with this secular shift in the center of gravity of economic might, a dispersal of geopolitical power is occurring giving rise to several pressing security challenges.

Sustained fast economic growth is not manifest destiny. Already, we see China's growth slowing from two digits to 7% or less; India is way down a similar path and the relative stagnation of the Japanese economy continues to run its long course. The broad consequences stemming from these tamed growth prospects defy definition.

Looking ahead, the main economic policy challenges that will confront Asian leaders will be to preserve the stability that has underpinned regional prosperity, to maintain an environment conducive to trade and investments and encourage domestic consumption. In this regard, we can take comfort from the resilience demonstrated by Asian countries during the 2008 global financial crisis. Although the external shocks stemming from the global financial crisis hit the region hard, the decline in output was shallower, the recovery was more rapid, and the cumulative output loss was smaller in comparison to other regions. Moreover, appropriate prudential policies ensured Asia's financial sector remained stable throughout this crisis.

China's growing assertiveness in establishing its dominion over a significant portion of its periphery raises geopolitical concerns. Political regional institutions and stability-enhancing mechanisms to mitigate and manage conflict within the region remain weak and inchoate, in sharp contrast to the extensive networks of economic arrangements that facilitate regional trade. In this day and age, China cannot implement a Western Pacific version of the Monroe Doctrine without encounter stiff opposition. The major challenges will therefore consist in defusing the destabilising security competition between China and major neighbouring countries, notably Japan and India, in preventing a lethal confrontation between China and the United States and avoiding the "Finlandization" of the countries on the littorals of the China seas.

With Success Comes Responsibilities

The rise of the share of East Asia economies in total world exports has been one of the defining features of the global economy in recent decades. Starting with Japan in the 1970s, it is undeniable that the economic success achieved by many Asian economies is tributary to the liberal investment, trade and monetary regime and the rule of law that underpins it which has been implemented by Western countries under U.S. leadership. The accession of China to the World Trade Organization in 2001 not only facilitated access to the large European and North American markets but was used by Chinese leaders to legitimate many reforms.

A major step in aligning the global governance architecture to the significant shift in the center of gravity of global economic power was taken in 2008 with the formation of the Group of Twenty (G20). Five Asian countries are member of the G20 which is destined to be a "premier forum for our international economic cooperation."[1] At the outset, the G20 was instrumental in ensuring that the global financial crisis did not cause a second Great Depression. It injected unprecedented liquidity into the world economy through coordinated national actions, including some $5 trillion in stimulus at the London Summit of April 2009. It reaffirmed the International Monetary Fund (IMF) bilateral and multilateral surveillance role and its function of international lender of last resort, created the Financial Stability Board with a mandate to develop new regulatory standards for systemically important financial institutions, and insisted on new bank capital account requirements under the Basel III agreement. Its members agreed to "standstill" provisions to avoid a recurrence of the ruinous beggar-thy-neighbor policies of the 1930s. The changes made to representation in the IMF and the World Bank agreed in November 2010 at the Seoul Summit better reflect the relative weight of members in the world economy; it assuredly gives China a more authoritative voice in the setting of policy directions.

China has to varying degrees upheld, accepted or adapted to prevailing structures and norms of the international system, except when they clash with its Westphalian conception of the world, or might create serious problems domestically. On balance, China has deepened and expanded its formal commitments to many international norms, especially in areas such as trade, nuclear non-proliferation and the management of non-traditional security threats such as pandemics. The engagement of the Chinese navy in joint anti-piracy operations with NATO navies in the Gulf of Aden and the Coast of Africa show that it is not allergic to collective actions when congruent with its broad interests.

Since the last four years, the momentum for significant reforms of major international financial institutions has evaporated, victim to

---

1 Leaders declaration at the Pittsburgh G20 meeting, 2009.

the G20 heterogeneous composition and the unwillingness of established members to diminish their standing within the governance structures. Changes to the "political" world governance institutions are prisoners of a similar status protective vise. Membership of the International Energy Agency (IEA) is limited to OECD members. The conspicuous absence of China, India and Indonesia, despite their huge imports of hydrocarbons, weakens the capacity of this multilateral institution to facilitate cooperation between energy-consuming countries. More broadly, it is accepted that institutions like the UN Security Council are in need of reform if they are to retain their credibility. Demands by India and Japan for a permanent membership on the UN Security Council have been actively opposed by China which is in a position to smoother proposals to change the composition and workings of this premier organ of world governance by virtue of its status on the Council.

Paradoxically, the major casualty from the rise of the economic might of emerging economies has been multilateral trade liberalization. The stance adopted by the major emerging market economies, notably Brazil, China and India, during the Doha Round of multilateral trade negotiations which started in November 2001, have not only played a part in the historic failure to reach an agreement but comforted many leaders in developed economies in the idea that the WTO multilateral approach was lopsided and that it no longer served their interests. And why should Western economies promote the economic interdependence that sustains overall growth but simultaneously produce geopolitical rivals? The response to this contemporary policy dilemma has been a systematic drive by major industrialized economies to eschew the WTO multilateral regime in favour of bilateral and regional free trade agreements. The United States has been particularly active on this front which, in turn, spurred a stampede by other countries to reach similar agreements in order to immunize their economies from the cost of trade diversion that is bound to ensue.

The Coming Inflexion in the Economic Trajectory

The rapid ascendancy of Asia as an economic and political force in global world affairs has lured many to underestimate the huge challenges that beset the Asian economic engines and to posit that current economic trends would simply continue. While it is reasonable to assume that Asian economic growth still has a way to go, it remains that the long-term social and economic foundations of growth in both China and India are more fragile than is generally recognized.

Projections concerning growth in China must contend with the fact that the conditions that fuelled its long period of rapid economic growth are fading. Between 2000 and 2015, the Chinese working-age population will have grown by 103 million, a surge that exerted downward pressure on wages and supercharged its export competitiveness. From 2015 to 2030, China working-age population will shrink by 69 million, with the opposite effects. More than 50% of China's population is now living in cities, indicating that it has largely exhausted its surplus labor from rural areas. The inexorable contraction in the labor force means that China will grow old before it grows rich, at least in per capita terms. A similar reversal is occurring with respect to the profitability of investments in machines and infrastructure: according to the IMF, capacity utilization has fallen from about 90% in 2000 to around 60% in 2011.

Chinese authorities are cognizant of the urgency "to stand up to the test of striding over the middle-income trap".[2] This can only be accomplished through rebalancing the sources of growth. The investment-driven growth has run its course, leading to worrying inefficiencies in the use of resources, a property bubble and adverse financial consequences. Moreover, it would be imprudent to rely on a further rapid expansion of the trade surplus to support the domestic economy. The transition to a more consumption-oriented growth has the added benefits of slowing the pace of widening income inequality and improving human welfare through more robust job creation and a more balanced development between coastal and inland regions. If successful, this rebalancing would reduce global economic imbalances and reduce upward pressure on the price of several commodities. But let's not be under any illusion, the policy challenges these new circumstances bring are of a different order of magnitude in complexity than what was the case in earlier periods.

---

2 Executive Vice Premier Zhang Goali, June 6th, 2013.

India also risks remaining stuck in the middle-income trap, unless it can mobilize the will and social consensus needed to adopt and implement appropriate policies. Contrary to China, India's demography is favorable and its dependency ratios are falling. This "demographic dividend" will be wasted if India fails to ensure that its young population is educated and has access to adequate healthcare and nutrition. To date, New Delhi policies regarding human capital development have been a miserable failure, if not in intent, for sure in implementation. The emergence of dynamic states growing at or near double-digit rates offers some comfort that India may gradually rid itself of the stifling regulations and rigid labor market institutions through power-sharing arrangements more typical of a mature federation.

Clouds on the Horizon

History teaches that polities seek power and status commensurate with their wealth. Increasing military expenditures, conflicting territorial and maritime disputes coupled to the fact that five of the eight declared nuclear states are in or border Asia are affecting regional security dynamics. The presence of three major Asian powers which actively compete with each other for influence and leadership in the region is fraught with risks, particularly since they still harbor resentment between each other. This general state of affairs renders the continued pursuit of a stable balance of power an absolute priority for Asian countries. Whether the competition between China and the United States for regional hegemony can be managed peacefully will remain a major source of concern. Clearly, the United States is seen as the only power that can contain China's, but no Asian country wants to be forced to choose side.

The Natural Resources Supply Imperative

The rapid rise of China and India will continue to have profound implications for the world economy in the decades ahead. In particular, their skinny endowment in natural resources in relation to their huge requirements and their dependence on seaborne supply have several consequences in the region and globally. It translates into relatively high world commodity prices and a range of actions to secure an abundant and stable supply of natural resources which are often pregnant with serious destabilizing effects.

From Japan to Southeast Asia, countries are islands or archipelagos while others, such as China, India, South Korea and Vietnam, have long coastlines. China has been assertive in claiming "ownership" of islands, giving rise to many disputes over territorial limits, continental shelf claims, Exclusive Economic Zone (EZZ) boundaries and other offshore issues. The driving factors often find their roots in domestic issues. For instance, the large increase in per capital consumption of halieutical products by the population of China coupled with the fact that overfishing and heavy pollution in inshore waters has led to a rapid depletion of these resources which used to account for more than 50% of the supply means that the strong demand can only be met by increased catches in the offshore waters. As these waters are often located in neighboring countries EEZs or disputed territory, the stage is set for repeated clashes between fisherman and Coast Guard authorities, fueling tensions.

The vulnerability of the hydrocarbon supply lines is another source of security concerns: Japan is almost completely dependent on seaborne imports; China and India import 90% of their needs by sea. The issue is that this traffic must pass through the Strait of Malacca and relies on the U.S. Navy to patrol and secure the Indo-Pacific sea lanes, a situation not totally satisfactory from a Chinese security perspective. China main strategic challenge is to maintain access to the Indian Ocean, both in peacetime and in wartime; a concern exacerbated by its conviction that India's current and expanding naval capabilities could easily curtail merchant and navy movements. In order to reduce its vulnerability, China has embarked on a comprehensive program aimed at circumventing the need to transit through vulnerable chocking points. Its strategic initiatives include the construction of ports and overland transportation routes through Pakistan and Myanmar, the promotion of trade and investment to reinforce economic integration through bilateral cooperation treaties and the construction of networks of roads and ports to facilitate commerce with China. Not surprisingly, New Delhi has been alarmed by the Beijing concerted actions which is viewed as expansionist and aimed at encircling India. The third consequence arising from the preoccupation with the security of supply is China's commitment to a major build-up of its naval capabilities.

An Arms Race in the Making?

China is building military forces in the Western Pacific that challenge the U.S. maritime supremacy. Independent assessments of China's ability to project naval power indicate that the new capabilities are mainly limited to offshore waters, not blue-water where the United States has no rival. The potency of the modernization plans of the Chinese navy is nevertheless very serious. Per design, it could eventually deny the U.S. Navy and its allies easy access to significant areas of the Western Pacific, allow China to exert control over Taiwan, should it be called for, and to establish its domination over the substantial oil and gas resources that lie in the ocean beds of the East and South China seas.

China's modernization of its navy has spurred actions in the Asian countries most vulnerable to China's assertiveness. This has taken the form of substantial investments in the acquisition of naval capabilities, to the conduct of naval exercises with the U.S. Navy, the conclusion of revitalized bilateral security alliances with the United States and the establishment of political and security relationships with India, Indonesia, Malaysia and Vietnam.

Even though China has not been involved in armed conflict with a neighbour since the Sino-Vietnam War of 1979, several flashpoints could rapidly enflame and raise tensions to the level of armed conflicts[3]. China's bellicose actions in the diplomatic spat with Japan over the disputed Diaoyu/Senkaku Islands and with the Philippines and Vietnam over the Spratly Islands are seen as a harbinger of things to come. The fear is that tit-for-tat actions spiral out of control even if some of them in and of themselves have little practical consequences. China's declaration of an Air Defence Identification Zone (ADIZ) over a large section of the East China Sea, including the Diaoyu/Senkaku Islands, is a case in point. In international law, ADIZ do not necessarily correspond to territorial

3 Previous military conflicts subsequent to the Korean War include the Taiwan Strait Crises of 1954 and 1958, the Indian border clash of 1962 and the conflict with the USSR along the Ussuri River in 1969-71. All these conflicts were in China's immediate periphery.

limits; for example, Canada's ADIZ covers half of the Artic Archipelago. The situation would become much more problematic if China unitarily declared an ADIZ over the entire South China Sea. The suspension of rare earth exports to Japan following a fall 2010 incident in the East China Sea shows China will not hesitate to use its economic might to impose its will. China's history of intimidating energy companies seeking contracts with Vietnam to pursue oil and gas exploration in the South China Sea add ballast to these concerns.

The importance ASEAN, Australia, Japan, South Korea and the United States have been giving to their relations with India is a reflection of the fears China has stroke in the region. Moreover, India's democratic polity is a fundamental value, a character that makes it a desirable partner for many Asian countries, the USA and other democratic countries, despite its often chaotic and unpredictable workings. After decades of estrangement, the rapprochement between the United States and India is significant even though it has and continues to be hampered by the tangled relationships with Pakistan[4], uncertainties concerning the aftermath of the Afghanistan military expedition and conflicting geopolitical goals. The geostrategic value of India is that of a counterweight to China's rise; however, New Delhi is circumspect about being seen by Beijing in that role.

Neither Allies nor Enemies

U.S.-China relations are undoubtedly one of the most potent bilateral relationships in the world. If its rise is sustained, it is likely that China will soon pose a decisive challenge to U.S. primacy in Asia. The prognostics on the future of Sino-American relations vary from the cautious to the optimistic. Kevin Rudd, cautions "history is not overburdened with examples of how such transitions in geopolitical and geo-economic realities have been accommodated peacefully"[5], while Henri Kissinger pragmatically suggests that "the U.S.-Chinese relationship should not be

---

4 Talbott, Strobe, "Engaging India, Diplomacy, Democracy and the Bomb", Brookings Institution Press, 2004.

5 Kevin Rudd, Remarks at the 70th Morrison Lecture, Australia 2011. Mr. Rudd is a former Australian Foreign Minister.

considered as a zero-sum game, nor can the emergence of a prosperous and powerful China be assumed in itself to be an American strategic defeat"[6]. Paradoxically, the United States involvement in Asia could be seen by all major actors, including China, as a constructive force preventing rivalry between Asian powers from spiralling out of control. The prevalent view held by Asian leaders is that the United States has underwritten the long period of peace, security and stability in the region which has undergirded its prosperity. It is often forgotten that one of the U.S. trump cards in Asia is that, contrary to all other powers jockeying for position, it has no territorial ambitions in the area. Clearly, defending strict adherence to the UN Law of the Sea Convention does not carry the same stigma as offensive actions to assert one's ownership of disputed territories[7].

There exists, nevertheless, numerous potential flashpoints. Tensions arising from the territorial disputes with China, the status of Taiwan or from lethal provocations or collapse of North Korea, could easily escalate since the United States is often bound by a security alliance with aggrieved countries. The risks of political missteps that would create serious tensions and have lasting economic consequences are aggravated by persistent doubts regarding the ability of the United States to muster sufficient financial, military and soft power to be considered the *primus inter pares* within the region, particularly by its "emerging giants". Comments by Asian analysts that Beijing appears to have concluded that the United States is on an irreversible path of decline and by European officials to the effect that their Chinese counterparts exhibit an uncompromising attitude in their encounters indicate that the likelihood of a serious miscalculation is increasing. These are compounded by the belief that Asian countries will hesitate to align closely with the United States should a limited conflict with China occur for fear of compromising the economic benefits they derive from their commercial intercourse with China. This cautious standing is also prevalent in India despite the prevailing consensus

---

6 Henri Kissinger, "The Future of U.S.-Chinese Relations", Foreign Affairs, March/April 2012.

7 See statement of Secretary Clinton at the 2010 annual meeting of the ASEAN Regional Forum and Bader J.A., "Obama and China's Rise—An insider account of America's Asia Strategy", Brookings 2012.

that it would never accept a China-centric Asia. This calculus is not peculiar to Asia. How to profit from China's huge markets without becoming vassals of its considerable economic power is a thorny issue in all capitals, including for Washington. These hesitations confirm that, for good or for ill, China remains the central strategic focus of Asia. This puts a premium on the quality and continuity of an effective institutional dialogue between China and United States at the highest levels, a process which, according to former U.S. Secretary of Defense, Robert Gates, has too often been held hostage to the vagaries of political decisions.[8]

An Uncertain World

The global dominance of Asia cannot be assumed as simply inevitable. China, India and Japan are confronted by an array of domestic challenges with little resolution in sight. Conversely, the capacity of the United States and Europe to rebound and embark on a growth path are too heavily discounted. The shale oil and gas phenomena and the re-shoring of manufacturing brought about, in part, by advanced technologies, are occurring; they are not figments of imagination. It is also worth keeping in mind that, in terms of output, the European Community and North American GDP only needs to increase by 1.5% to match that of China growing at 7%.

Nor should it be assumed to be a foregone outcome that tensions in the Asia-Pacific will reach the boiling point and escalate into a regional outburst of catastrophic magnitude arresting the spreading of prosperity across Asia. Unlike the situation that prevailed during the Cold War where trade relations between the Soviet and Western Blocks were virtually non-existent, Asia, especially China, is deeply integrated into the world economy. This reality is bound to weight in any calculus of the consequences of expanding a skirmish into a conflict, although we can never be certain that "cooler heads" will always prevail.

---

8 Robert M. Gates, *Duty: Memoirs of a Secretary at War*, 2014.

SHAUKAT AZIZ

Shaukat Aziz, Former Prime Minister of Pakistan (2004-2007), and Former Executive Vice-President, Citibank, was elected as Prime Minister of Pakistan and served from 2004-2007, following five years as Finance Minister from 1999. After graduating from Gordon College, Rawalpindi in 1967, Mr. Aziz gained a MBA degree from the Institute of Business Administration, University of Karachi. An internship at Citibank marked the beginning of a 30 years career in global finance. Having presided over impressive economic growth in his country, Mr. Aziz offers an expert view and is a frequent speaker on the challenges facing the world including structural reforms, diplomacy, geopolitics and security.

SUSTAINABLE GROWTH AND GLOBAL POLITICAL RISKS

Solid economic growth and a country's political stability are inextricably linked. While in the short term the relationship between them may not be as clear-cut, a vibrant policy framework and reform agenda, supported by good governance for maximum impact, are the corner stones for building sustainable economic growth and giving a country a meaningful, enduring boost. Even then, global crises and geopolitical shocks can disrupt any country's progress, and countries must be able to deal with the repercussions of unpredictable events through nimble contingency planning.

How do We Define Sustainable Growth?

A country's development must encompass more than financial growth and high GDP numbers—growth should be equitable, geared towards improving quality of life, services and infrastructure, and environment-friendly, with future generations in mind.

Economic transformation through structural reforms and strong, forward-looking leadership is crucial for any nation that wishes to boost growth. This should be steered by a leader who has the ability to focus on more than the short term political cycle. A reform agenda of deregulation, liberalization and privatization are key to creating an enabling environment for growth. Strong, independent regulating bodies that can protect public interest are also necessary.

No country, whether developing or developed, is immune from this need to reform. It is a continuous, evolving process, critical for adapting a country to its ever-changing environment. However, for the purposes of this article, I will focus more on the relationship between growth and risk in developing countries.

However good the intentions and reform agenda of a government, its policy implementation can be hampered by crises, non state actors and global events. In today's globalised world, no nation can be looked at in isolation.

All states are vulnerable to geopolitical events and crises that are usually entirely out of their control. Territorial disputes, such as those in the Middle East, will cause damage to growth for both the countries involved and, often, their trade partners. The existence of historical border disputes or threats from other countries can mean that a large part of a country's budget is eaten up by defense building, and cannot be reinvested to encourage economic and infrastructural development.

Wars in the Gulf and the Middle East can cause the oil price to shoot up, because of the world's dependency on their energy supplies. Such a shock will affect the balance of payments of many countries, holding back growth and impeding progress.

It is sometimes hard to separate out political risks from economic ones, and the two are often interlinked. Both can have a corrosive effect on growth. Global economic crises, such as the financial crash in 2008, will affect many countries at once. In that particular case, it was more the developed world that was hit, but there were worldwide repercussions—the countries affected by the financial crisis have their hands tied in many ways on the global arena, because their economies are substantially weaker and they need to direct efforts to address their on challenges. The recent inability of the European Union to move fast in providing assistance to a crisis-ridden and near-bankrupt Ukraine is testament to this. Natural disasters, such as tsunamis, floods and earthquakes can also cause great unforeseen damage that will disrupt growth.

It is to ward against geopolitical shocks and economic crises that a prudent government would have a set of contingency plans in place—a buffer for the damages caused by unforeseen circumstances. This includes setting aside reserves for emergencies. Oil-dependent countries should have plans in place for conserving energy use in the event of an oil price hike, through adjusting prices and informing the public about how to save costs and conserve energy. There should also make provisions for a public program to protect the most vulnerable and poor in such a scenario.

Countries should also make contingency plans for the long run, to better prepare themselves for unforeseen geopolitical crises. Being dependent for your energy supply is unavoidable for most nations, but it makes them more vulnerable. The drive towards energy self-sufficiency, which has been actively pursued by some countries, is a way to break out of this and make them less prone to global risks. The United States has been working hard to become energy self-sufficient, ever since it saw how devastating the consequences of the 1973 oil shock were, when the Organization of Arab Petroleum Exporting Countries (OAPEC) announced an oil embargo against the United States, the United Kingdom, Canada, Japan and the Netherlands. The nominal price of oil quadrupled over the course of a few months. By 1974, 20% of all gas stations in the United States had no fuel at all. The self-sufficiency policy is working. In the next five years the United States—the world's biggest oil importer—will account for a third of new oil supplies, according to the International Energy Agency.

Wars and geopolitical maneuvering are nothing new, but today the world order is also changing and new threats are fast emerging, threatening peace and stability. Terrorism, new conflicts and growing concerns about the proliferation of weapons of mass destruction all pose significant global risks.

Both regionally and globally, the last decade of the twentieth century witnessed momentous changes—the emergence of unipolarity with the end of the Cold War, the spread of democracy, the formation of new geopolitical blocks and the growth of free market economies.

Against this background, the twenty first century was expected to be the harbinger of peace, progress and prosperity. Nevertheless, such hopes have been tempered by a new realism. The September 11 attacks on the World Trade Centre made the wide reaching, global threat of terrorism painfully clear to people around the world. Since then, new tensions have emerged that risk tipping into conflict, such as the territorial disputes in the South China Sea and mounting tensions in the Ukraine and Venezuela. The Middle East continues to be a major issue with global implications, and the Arab Spring countries have had great difficulties in regaining order and stability since.

But not only global conflict and maneuvering count as political risk. Government coups and infighting, civil unrest and problems with law and order present high risks. These tend to affect poorer, developing countries, yet neither are more developed ones immune to political risk. The uncertainty brought about by a new party coming into power or not being clear about its policies can have an adverse effect anywhere, but for the purposes of this discussion I will focus more on the developing world.

The relationship between economic growth and political risk is a complex one. On the face of it, political instability does not necessarily hamper growth in the short term. When looking at the link between countries' political risk and their growth over the course of one year, there does not seem to be big difference between how the riskier countries fare compared with the stable ones.

The long term trend is more telling. If you look at the same relationship over the course of two decades, for example, the riskier countries usually lag behind in growth by up to 50% on average. Some examples, such as Angola, buck the trend, but for the most part a high level of political risk makes better growth unsustainable.

But it would be a mistake to draw a clear-cut causational relationship from high political risk to poor economic growth. Firstly, in many cases investment does not immediately dry up because countries are unstable. In fact, over the past few years the trend has been for investors to seek out high risk opportunities in emerging markets, in the hope of high yields.

Neither does the relationship only work in one direction. Poor economic performance, high unemployment and poverty can cause instability and political risk. Weak governance can create poor growth through bad management and make a country vulnerable to instability.

A history of political upheaval or cases where leaders are attacked or imprisoned are both a symptom and a contributing factor to instability. As leaders do not have any certainty about what their future will be once they are out of government, they have more incentive to hang on to power for longer and to tighten their grip on the country. This can lead to poor management, corruption and irrational or unexpected policy making, which hampers growth and investment. In the case of a coup, most countries will either refuse to deal with a military government, or use sanctions to try and contain it.

But by far the greatest destabilizer in the Middle East, Central and South Asia and now increasingly Africa has been the growth of terrorism and the threat of non-state actors who increasingly disrupt the system, attacking government bases and civilians and disrupting trade routes. They create a dangerous, unstable climate in which growth cannot flourish and encourage the government to redirect resources to combat the threat. Policies are harder to implement and the state loses part of its effectiveness. Terrorism brings threats to water, food, energy supply and the country's security.

Terrorism and extremism are both factors of deprivation. They spread by preying on poverty and a nation's disillusionment with ineffective governance. It is when deprivation reaches a stage where people they feel they are not heard that they are vulnerable to being converted to extreme causes.

So what can be done? Even when a country is faced with adversity, poor economic performance can be minimized through good hip, structural reforms, continuity and consistency of policy, acy and investing in the country's future potential. I will proceed to describe these in turn.

Many developing countries in the Middle East and Asia have strong demographics, a rising young population with a high capacity to work hard. These countries needs world-class leadership to unlock their full potential. It needs people in charge who are qualified, have exposure to the world, are honest and transparent. There is an important distinction between true leaders and politicians—the former worry about the next generation, the latter about the next election. Short-term goals will encourage poor policy decisions that may not ultimately be in the country's interests.

A good leader should have a helicopter-like quality, steering over the scene, hovering to make sure everything is under control, fixing emergencies as they happen and quickly rising up again. The argument against micromanaging applies just as much to countries as it does to running a company.

Good, effective governance is a critical element of statecraft, and it is characterized by several important values, most notably transparency, accountability and the rule of law. It is the responsibility of a good leader to create these conditions.

Structural reforms are necessary for any country that wishes to transform its economy. Deregulation, liberalization and privatization should lay the groundwork for achieving this. Creating a free market and opening up a country to foreign investment will help adapt it to the 21st century. It is also important to encourage innovation in technology, telecommunications and services, instead of relying only on manufacturing to boost growth, as well as stripping away institutional barriers to productivity, encouraging transparency and empowering women will all help to unleash a country's economic potential. Having consistent policies will foster stability and boost investor confidence. Inconsistency and uncertainty are sure ways to drive away investment.

The chance of long term growth and the continuation of reform will be boosted through investment in human capital, providing people with education, skills and healthcare. This is needed to increase a country's competitiveness through better workers, management and innovators.

The political process often also needs reform to eliminate gridlock and facilitate growth. In many emerging countries, the democratic structures are still relatively young and developing. Political adversaries can focus more on infighting and winning the next election than legislating and effectively implementing policy, leading to gridlock.

Sometimes an ineffective and stagnant democratic process can prompt the military or other stakeholders to intervene and seize control. Even though this can make policy implementation more effective in the short term, in the long run it will cause significant damage. This is because stability is key to building healthy, functioning institutions and encouraging investment. Coups hurt the democratic processes that are in place and set a dangerous precedent for uncertainty. Democratic rule is the best way to lay the foundations for a sustainable system in the long term. A country must have a credible set of checks and balances in place through an effective Parliament and judiciary that will allow the government to function.

In the long term, efforts must be made to lower global political risk and the threat of conflict, by using diplomacy and encouraging linkages and interdependencies between countries. Negotiations should be used to minimize political risks of territorial disputes and potential escalation into confrontation.

Negotiations will be most effective when the countries in question should have mutual interests. That way, when tensions do surface, both sides will work them out diplomatically because there are too many interests at stake. Common approaches on global issues and the existence of common adversaries—whether a particular country or non state actors, as in the War on Terror, will also strengthen ties between nations and minimize the risk of conflict between them. Post 9/11 co-operation and co-ordination was an excellent example of how nations can work together for a common goal.

Trade and energy cooperation are good ways of creating inter-dependencies and linkages between countries, which is vital for peace, and the best way for even historical rivals to coexist. Free trade agreements and developing a framework for intra-regional cooperation will create solid ties. Examples of energy cooperation include oil and gas pipelines, electricity grids across borders, emission reduction agreements and sharing research into alternative energy. International guidelines can help develop energy in a sustainable and safe way—the International Energy Agency (IEA) has published a set of 'Golden Rules' for developing the world's gas resources.

These stress the importance of full transparency, measuring and monitoring of environmental impacts and engagement with local communities, the careful choice of drilling sites and measures to prevent any leaks from wells into nearby aquifers, rigorous assessment and monitoring of water requirements and of waste water, measures to target zero venting and minimal flaring of gas, improved project planning and regulatory control.

International nuclear treaties can also play a part in controlling nuclear weapons buildup and not letting nuclear races between rivals spiral, thus lowering that political risk.

That said, credible defense policies and an effective internal security system and counter terrorism capacity are needed to protect the country's borders and maintain its sovereignty. Even if force is never used, its presence and the potential to use it can help a country against the threat of external intervention.

When bilateral diplomacy fails and tensions escalate, multilateral institutions, such as the United Nations, the EU, ASEAN and others, can play a mediating role in resolving potential crises. For developing countries facing economic problems, the International Monetary Fund and the World Bank play a role in giving them a life line. However, not only are such institutions in need of further reform, developing nations should aim to manage their progress themselves, because the final onus for its success will rest on them.

Rapid expansion as a result of tapping into natural resources can bring substantial short term growth but, unless it is well managed, it will not be sustainable in the long run. Countries with natural resources should strive to invest the income from them so that future generations can continue to reap their benefits—as in the example of Norway.

When considering trying to boost their country's growth levels, leaders must adapt to the realities of the 21st century and the environmental risks we all face, and focus their attention not only on growth, but on making sure that the environment is not damaged further in the process.

Exploiting the world's vast resources is vital for development, and their use was central to the Industrial Revolution and the exponential economic growth of those industrial countries. The story is being repeated in the emerging markets today. But not only is the number of these resources finite, the risks to the environment associated with them are substantial. According to the UN Panel on Climate Change, the globe's temperature is already 1-2 degrees centigrade higher than it was prior to the Industrial Revolution and weather patterns have been affected. The panel estimated that, unless growth in carbon emissions is halted and reversed, the world's temperature will increase by another 2 degrees centigrade within 20 or 30 years. This is likely to have catastrophic effects on the world's environment, weather and eco-systems.

Investing in alternative energy sources is a good way of encouraging growth for the future. Germany has been a world leader in this. But such development usually requires substantial investment and a healthy economy, which many countries struggle with. Hydro power is the cheapest energy source, but its use is geographically limited and at times the environmental impacts are significant. Wind and solar power have become cheaper but they still require generous subsidies to be competitive. However, headway has been made in recent years in lowering solar technology costs—Swanson's Law shows the steep drop in cost of solar cells, suggesting that they effectively halve every three years. However, the cost of installing a solar infrastructure is still very high. But this is something that can be a significant way of boosting development in the future, and minimizing a country's exposure to geopolitical shocks.

In short, political risks and their effects may come and go, but good governance, structural reforms and successful policy implementation are the key factors that will help a country develop its potential for long term, stable, equitable and environmentally-friendly growth.

It is the responsibility of every government to encourage growth and distribute its benefits in an equitable manner that helps boost living standards, works to eradicate poverty, contain sources of unrest and instability, thus laying the foundations for future generations to flourish. This will not only help manage existing political risks and crises, but also protect the country from the development of future risks.

ADAM STEINHOUSE

Adam Steinhouse is an international European Union consultant and affiliated professor at the École nationale d'administration publique (ENAP) in Canada. He was formerly Head of the School of European Studies at the UK National School of Government and taught European Politics at the universities of Oxford, Cambridge and the LSE, and was a commentator for the BBC and CNN on European and North American affairs. His book, Workers' Participation in Post-Liberation France, was published by Lexington Books. Born in Montreal, Adam Steinhouse graduated with a BA from Harvard University and a DPhil from the University of Oxford.

WHERE NEXT FOR EUROPEAN ECONOMIC INTEGRATION?

I taught a course for civil servants recently in Madrid and suddenly at one point their cellphones buzzed with a text announcing an immediate 5% cut in their salaries. Outside, in the Puerta del Sol, workers protested at job losses and cutbacks in the health sector. This news of declining living standards and growing unemployment features daily in the eurozone and beyond. In the increased regulation of the European economy and in the discussion of austerity versus growth policies, there seems to be less access for people's voices. The path of European economic integration was meant in part to address social concerns. What has gone wrong and what is the way forward?

European integration started from the almost revolutionary principle that nations had to cede sovereignty to promote peace and prosperity. Jean Monnet said that the proposals for the first treaty which created the European Coal and Steel Community (the Paris Treaty of 1951) would "provide a basis for the building of a new Europe through the concrete achievement of a supranational regime within a limited but controlling area of economic effort... The indispensable first principle of these proposals is the abnegation of sovereignty in a limited but decisive field." The same six countries which signed the first treaty then went on to agree the Messina Declaration in 1955: "The governments of the Federal Republic of Germany, Belgium, France, Italy, Luxembourg and the Netherlands believe the time has come to take a new step on the road of European construction. They are of the opinion that these objectives should be achieved first of all in the economic sphere. They believe that the establishment of a united Europe must be achieved through the development of common institutions, the progressive fusion of national economies, the creation of a common market, and the gradual harmonisation of their social policies. Such an agenda seems indispensable to them if Europe is to preserve the standing which she has in the world, to restore her influence and her prestige, and to improve steadily the living standards of her population."

The outline of the future European Union could be seen in the specific objectives of the "Common Market": The Messina declaration called not only for the "suppression of obstacles to trade in relations between participating countries", but for the coordination of monetary policies and free circulation of labour. It even called for social harmonisation, particularly in relation to the length of the working day: the seeds of the Working Time Directive were sown in Sicily in 1955. The Messina Declaration invited the United Kingdom to participate in the discussions that followed and that resulted in the two Treaties of Rome. UK representatives, at official level, did participate in the Spaak committee for a few months, but withdrew in November 1955, having failed to win safeguards for intergovernmentalism against the supranational approach of "the six". The European Economic Community (EEC) and Euratom Treaties were signed on 25 March 1957 and came into effect, following ratification, on 1 January 1958.

The preamble of the Treaty of Rome started with the undertaking by the member states that they were "determined to lay the foundations of an ever-closer union among the peoples of Europe." The meaning of "ever closer union" was never spelled out—the phrase does suggest a process of constant integration, and political unity, in one form or another, was the declared goal of the founders of the European Union. The phrase was specifically rejected by current British prime minister David Cameron in a speech in London in January 2013, in what he called a heretical proposition: "We believe in a flexible union of free member states who share treaties and institutions and pursue together the ideal of co-operation. This vision of flexibility and cooperation is not the same as those who want to build an ever closer political union —but it is just as valid."

Another view of the term, which might also serve as a definition of the European "community method", is that it is simply the process of continually harmonising standards and processes to make them more effective, for example to eliminate barriers. Walter Hallstein, a German lawyer and diplomat who became the European Commission's first President in 1958, famously likened Europe to a bicycle: it has to go forward, or it will fall over.

The tools to achieve the lofty objectives set out in the preamble to the Treaty of Rome were a set of policies. These went far beyond the arrangements of a free trade area, where internal tariffs are removed, or even of a customs union, where a common external tariff is imposed. Above all, the provisions for an internal market characterised by "the abolition, as between member states, of obstacles to freedom of movement for [goods], persons, services and capital" meant that something more than a "Common Market" was on the cards. Taken together with the institutions needed to make these freedoms a reality, the Treaty of Rome created something that already had, necessarily, many of the features of a state.

By the mid-1980s, following the accession of the United Kingdom, Ireland and Denmark in 1973 and of Greece in 1981, and with the accession of Spain and Portugal imminent, European leaders decided that reform of the institutions and policies of the EEC had become imperative. Hidden barriers to trade were obstructing the completion of the Single European Market programme. With cautious endorsement from the UK's Prime Minister, Mrs. Thatcher,

European governments commenced what was to be the first of many treaty revisions. The Single European Act, signed in 1986, pushed for completion of the internal (or single) market by 1992, through measures achieved particularly by the extension of qualified majority voting in Council. A paradox lay at the heart of the Single European Act and of the "1992" project for a true internal market that it set out to achieve. For its aim was the world's biggest market economy, an area of liberalisation and competition. Yet the achievement of that market economy depended on regulation and supervision: hence the need for extensive changes to legislative procedures. Europe needed QMV so that laws could be passed to enable the institutions of the European Community to uphold and enforce the single market. The treaty would mark a crucial step in the loss of national sovereignty, as a single country could no longer veto a change in the rules of the European internal market.

The irony of regulation implemented to achieve a free market was deepened by the determination of the European Commission, led by its influential president of the time, Jacques Delors, to see two "flanking" measures to the programme of completion of the internal market. The first was "compensatory" in nature: the need for a social charter, a series of social measures to protect workers in the newly liberalised and expanded internal market. The second was a reinforcing measure: the need for currency stability or, better still, just one currency. These initiatives would lead to two of the big arguments that surrounded the biggest treaty revision of all: Maastricht, signed in 1992.

The Community Method

The European Union remains the legacy of the Treaties of Paris and Rome, but Maastricht gave it the shape and content that we recognise today, as well as its name. The Maastricht Treaty was drafted in a world remarkably different to that of the Single European Act just six years earlier. It was shaped in the aftermath of the collapse of the Berlin Wall and the reunification of Germany, with a new focus on citizens' rights, justice and foreign policy. Apart from these new policies in external and home affairs and significant institutional changes, there were two other major developments: European Monetary Union (EMU) and the Social Chapter.

The Single European Act had set itself the objective of creating a true internal market by 1992. But to create a true internal market, macroeconomic stability between member states was required, and for that to be achieved, exchange rate stability was an essential first step -- hence the exchange rate mechanism, always intended as a staging post to the euro. In the preamble of the Maastricht Treaty, the member states resolved "to achieve the strengthening and the convergence of their economies and to establish an economic and monetary union including [...] a single and stable currency".

The treaty also contained the Social Chapter: eleven member states agreed to a whole range of measures relating to protection of workers' rights, equal pay and social exclusion. After protracted negotiations, the UK opted out of the Social Chapter to the treaty, though the later government of Tony Blair rescinded this opt-out in 1997.

Since the signing of the Maastricht Treaty (almost coinciding with the history of the Conference of Montreal), the ethos of the European Union has remained committed to the community method and Hallstein's "bicycle metaphor". Give a strong central executive (the European Commission) exclusive right to propose new legislation, set it clear economic and political objectives and give it supranational powers. But ensure that it acts supranationally – that is, in the interests of all member states and the interest of the European Union as a whole, not in the interests of any state or group in particular. Leave to keep pedalling away for fifty-five years, working incrementally to remove barriers, harmonise, and integrate.

There are, however, a number of difficulties with the community method. It lacks transparency, owing in part to the working methods of the Commission and also because so much of the legislative process (in Council Working Groups and in trialogues between the Council, the Commission and the Parliament) takes place behind closed doors. Although the supranational aspect of the community method is potentially efficient, because it entails a central body proposing legislation and defending its proposals against the depredations of member states and the parliament, it is not particularly sensitive to national interests. It is this lack of sensitivity to the particular circumstances of certain member states, particularly their labour markets and social policies, that has characterised the recent period since the advent of the economic crisis in 2007-08.

The principal focus of the EU in the containment of the crisis has centred understandably on financial stability and risks. Jacques de Larosière, former Governor of the Banque de France, headed a group which published a key report in 2009 for the European Commission on financial supervision in the European Union. De Larosière recognised that the EU framework of financial and regulatory supervision remained seriously fragmented and he advocated three major areas of reform, all of which have come to pass: a new regulatory agenda to improve risk management; stronger coordinated supervision for financial actors; effective crisis management procedures. The European response in the past five years has seen the establishment of the European Systemic Risk Board and three European Supervisory Authorities (ESAs), in banking, insurance and securities markets, which are creating a single EU rule-book and drafting binding technical standards, which are then adopted by the European Commission, for firms in their respective fields. National supervisors will have to apply the rules properly, as ESAs have a power to investigate alleged breaches of European Union law. National supervisory authorities have lost national powers as decision making has been Europeanised, with the ESAs gathering more responsibilities and powers.[1] These developments have arguably deepened the single market, while removing power from individual member states.

There has also been rapid progress towards banking union within the eurozone, including the creation of the Single Supervisory Mechanism making the European Central Bank the common supervisor for the eurozone's largest banks. Mutualised resolution has also been established, with the Single Resolution Mechanism having just been agreed in March 2014 to deal with failing banks in the European banking union. The United Kingdom has stood to the sidelines in this process, with the UK Chancellor George Osborne stressing that there is a "remorseless logic" for a banking

---

1 I am grateful to Peter Parker for his guidance in this section; the conclusions are mine alone.

and fiscal union in the eurozone, but there is "no way" that Britain would be part of that union.

How to Accomodate Divergence

Over the last two decades the single market in financial services has been pursued by more and more harmonising legislation and greater efforts to move supervision to the EU level. EU agencies now take decisions involving a high level of discretion. Many of the regulations passed over the last five years have built-in review clauses and implementation assessments which will keep the Commission and national regulators busy in the coming period. But the decision-making process is highly technical, if not technocratic, and excludes those with more limited access, outside of governments. The European Trade Union Confederation, for example, contends that the concentration on financial stability in economic policy making has meant a less aggressive focus on reducing unemployment. The focus of policy making must therefore shift to the promotion of economic recovery and growth.

More than six million jobs were lost in the EU from 2008-2013. In the third quarter 2013, over 31 million people of all ages in the eurozone were either looking for jobs, willing to do so though unavailable, or else had given up. At the same time, wages have been falling or were frozen in Spain, Portugal, Ireland and Greece. Inappropriate macroeconomic policies and excessive austerity policies have had a significant impact on depressed economies. The implications of launching a single currency, especially the institutional asymmetries in EMU, were not sufficiently acknowledged by policy makers. In Harvard professor Peter Hall's work on varieties of capitalism, the Northern European / German model features innovation, coordinated wage bargaining, skills formation, export-led growth strategies; whereas the Southern European / Spanish model comprises the opposite, with demand-led growth strategies. The southern Europeans could not do what the northern Europeans did, because their choices were conditioned by built-up structures. The European Central Bank's one-size-fits-all monetary policy created destabilising imbalances in the eurozone. The incipient banking union was needed to break the vicious cycle of weak banks and debt-laden governments. Why didn't the banking union come earlier? The lack of attention to particular circumstances was built into the functioning of the community method. Eurozone governments' inability to agree a form of fiscal burden-sharing led to highly pro-cyclical fiscal policy in some countries and has prevented rapid action to address the region's banking sector problems, according to Simon Tilford, of the Centre for European Reform. Fiscal union remains unclear, but any such centralisation would demand even greater accountability at the EU level.

A new component in policy coordination, the surveillance of macroeconomic imbalances in member states, was put in place in 2011 with six EU legislative acts (the so-called "six-pack") to strengthen economic governance in the EU. Under the European Semester the member states submit their budgetary and reform plans in the early stages of their national budgetary processes. In the past, the member states coordinated their policy plans after the adoption of national budgets. With this shift in the timing of EU policy coordination, the Semester reduces the control of national parliaments over EMU-related policy making at the national level, while not so far granting any corresponding increase in the role of the European Parliament, as has noted the analyst Christian Deubner. Accountability remains, therefore, increasingly elusive.

The future of the European Union now rests not so much in further economic integration, but in how divergence within the eurozone can be accommodated. Economic and monetary union can be preserved by fiscal transfers from north to south. But can the electorates be convinced that they are part of a shared political entity, as happens in a federal state? The failure to preserve EMU would be more costly than the alternative, says Peter Hall. Growing inequality, high unemployment and increasing poverty undermine long-term growth and social and political stability.

ENERGY CHALLENGES

MARIA VAN DER HOEVEN

Maria van der Hoeven has served as Executive Director of the International Energy Agency (IEA) since September 2011. She has steered the IEA during a period of exceptional change in the global energy landscape, and is taking the initiative to address the challenges of global energy governance. Her priorities include building and formalising cooperation with the major emerging energy players of the 21st century, and also expanding energy access. Ms. van der Hoeven was formerly Minister of Economic Affairs of the Netherlands.

ENERGY FOUNDATION FOR THE NEXT ERA OF GROWTH

As the International Energy Agency (IEA) has said many times, greenhouse-gas emissions, two-thirds of which come from the energy sector, are still on a dangerous course that will not lead the world to the internationally agreed goal of limiting the rise in global temperatures to 2 degrees Celsius. While urgent action on the climate is necessary, it is by no means the only persistent energy sector issue requiring long-term solutions. A significant portion of the world's population, or about 1.3 billion people, lack access to modern energy—the most basic form of energy security. Moreover, high energy prices continue to create economic hardship around the world, and severely impact economic competitiveness in some sectors. Oil prices have averaged over $110/barrel since 2011, and such a sustained period of high prices is without parallel in oil market history. It is now more than five years after the onset of the worst economic recession since the 1930's, yet the recovery continues to be fragile and downside risks remain. In short, the classic "energy trilemma" of simultaneously achieving energy security, sustainability, and economic prosperity is now more pertinent then ever.

Shifting Patterns of Oil Production and Consumption

Oil was the focus fuel of *WEO-2013*, and IEA analysis reveals major changes in that sector. In 2012, we wrote that North American developments were helping to redraw the global energy map. Indeed, many of the changes we highlighted have only become more rapid and more pronounced over the past two years. Technology and high prices are unlocking new supplies of oil—but of course also gas—that were previously thought to be out of reach. Yet while unconventional production may have helped to usher in a "golden age" of gas, we should not overstate the potential of unconventional oil to provide an era of oil abundance. New supplies of unconventional oil, such as North American light-tight oil (LTO) and Canadian oil sands, will reduce OPEC's share of supply over the next decade. Other new sources will also contribute, such as increased natural gas liquids and deep-water offshore resources from Brazil. But the Middle East is still the only large source of low-cost oil. And we expect it to take back its role as the key source of oil supply growth from the mid-2020s.

One of the consequences of those changes is a transformed global product supply chain. New, non-OECD mega-refineries in West, South, and East Asia are challenging OECD refining economics, at least beyond the US and Canada. Their expanding reach is accelerating the globalisation of the product market, particularly in the case of refineries geared toward export. With a more global market comes not only the benefit of greater market flexibility in the dispatch of product supply, but also risks associated with longer supply chains, higher reliance on stocks to meet demand, diminished visibility in inventory levels, increased disruption risks, reduced market transparency and, possibly, greater price variation between key markets and also between seasonal peaks and troughs in demand.

The IEA's *Medium-Term Oil Market Report 2013*, released in May of last year, offers projections to 2018. As refinery capacity additions are forecast to increase faster than world demand over the medium term, the persistence of excess refining capacity is expected to weigh on refining margins, severely affecting the less efficient and older refineries in the world. The overall upgrading ratio gradually increases from 44% in 2012 to 47% in 2018 as new refineries focus mainly on heavy crude oil processing, mostly from the Middle East and Latin America. The capacity expansions in Asia and the Middle East, however, represent two distinct investment strategies. Whereas Asian capacity development is meant to service rapidly rising domestic demand, Middle East exporters (mostly in joint venture with OECD refiners or Chinese companies, and mostly in Saudi Arabia) are climbing the value chain and expanding into products and petrochemicals.

This has put OECD refiners—particularly in Europe—into a tight spot. Facing weak demand, tighter regulations, and an aging capital stock, these refiners have little choice but to increase their competitiveness through restructuring and consolidation. The refining sector in OECD Americas is undergoing a complete restructuring, with each regional district trying to optimise its crude slate between light domestic crude oil and heavy imported oil. High, sustained margins and the outlook for continued growth pushes North American refiners to invest in deep conversion and light oil processing. Recent developments in Spain and Portugal show that investment into deep conversion units can indeed present a profitable alternative to closures. Despite these efforts, the overcapacity that exists today is bound to force a continuation of the capacity shut-ins we have seen since 2008. Over that period, 15 European refineries have closed with a total capacity of 1.7 mb/d, and more are expected in the coming years. Japanese refiners will close around 800 kb/d by next year, in line with government regulations aimed at increasing conversion yields.

Looking out to 2035, the global refining sector is set to experience continued turbulence amidst declining OECD demand and Asian growth. The outlook for North America is helped by the increasing availability of local crude, but the benefits to refiners vary by location thanks to new supply sources and ongoing infrastructure constraints. Still, as the net North American requirement for imported crude all but disappears by 2035, the region becomes a large exporter of oil products. On the other hand, medium-term European difficulties are compounded to 2035 by declining local crude production (particularly from the North Sea), product demand that is heavily skewed towards diesel, and disappearing export markets for gasoline.

For the non-OECD, the longer outlook period also reveals new trends. Middle Eastern refining capacity additions, initially focused on boosting product exports, turn to meet domestic needs as regional demand rises to 2035. And Asia emerges as the unrivalled centre of global trade, drawing in a rising share of crude not only from the Middle East, but also from Russia, Africa, Latin America, and Canada. Massive additions to refining capacity are still not sufficient to meet regional demand, and both China and India are net oil product importers in 2035.

Pricing Differentials and Competitiveness

Oil is not alone. Supply and demand patterns are shifting across the fuel spectrum. At the nexus of supply and demand are energy prices, which have become a live issue in political debate—especially in terms of their impact on competitiveness. Where energy prices are high they have put pressure on household spending and import bills, but they have also generated demand- and supply-side responses—particularly where the those prices are highly variable across the globe.

Gas is a prime example. There has been a substantial widening of the gap between natural gas prices in North America, Europe and Asia, with some important effects on relative competitiveness. Gas prices in Europe are about three times those in the US, and in Japan they can be up to five times the US figure. Gas market and pricing reforms particularly in the Asia-Pacific region, as well as LNG exports from North America and elsewhere, can spur a loosening of contractual and pricing rigidities—a process that will be underway over the coming decades.

Long-term, oil-indexed gas contracts continue to dominate international gas trading, despite the fact that oil and gas are poor substitutes. And while long-term contracts can provide demand security for very expensive projects, they also make for less liquid, less flexible, and less integrated gas markets. The bulk of new LNG supplies will follow the same path, but an important and growing amount will not. North American spot contracts, and secondary re-exports from Europe and elsewhere, will play an increasing role. In the case of Asia, these flexible supplies can help provide liquidity to a developing Asian gas hub.[1]

Coping with Price Disparities and Sustainability: the Case for Efficiency

In most sectors, in most countries, energy is a relatively minor part of the calculation of competitiveness. But energy costs can be of crucial importance to energy-intensive industries, such as chemicals, aluminium, cement, iron and steel, paper, glass, and oil refining, particularly where the resulting goods are traded internationally. We focused on these sectors in our analysis to see how energy might influence the competitive landscape.

We found that in many emerging economies, particularly in Asia, strong growth in domestic demand for energy-intensive goods supports a swift rise in their production, accompanied by an expansion of exports. In the United States, relatively low energy costs also help to generate an increase in the US share of global exports of energy-intensive goods in the period to 2035.

By contrast, the European Union and Japan, both with relatively high energy costs, see sharp declines of -10% and -3%, respectively. This suggests that, at least among the OECD economies, energy price variations have clear potential to influence investment decisions and company strategies in these sectors.

Intensive action must start today. While critically important UN climate talks in Paris in 2015 will strive to agree on a long-term framework, effective measures will likely take at least 5 years to implement. Yet by 2020, global energy-related greenhouse-gas emissions are projected to be nearly 4 gigatonnes higher than a

---

1 In February 2013, the IEA released a report showing how that process can play out: IEA (2013), *Developing a Natural Gas Trading Hub in Asia*, Paris.

level consistent with attaining the 2 °C target. The IEA's *World Energy Outlook 2013* Special Report "Redrawing the Energy-Climate Map" presents a set of four proven policy actions that can deliver significant emissions reductions by 2020 and can help keep the door open to the 2°C reality. These include adopting targeted energy efficiency measures; limiting the least-efficient coal-fired power plants; reducing methane releases particularly through flaring; and partially phasing out fossil fuel subsidies. Critically, these measures can be implemented at zero net economic cost. They comprise approaches that are proven and feasible, without compromising energy security or relying on new technology.

Renewable Energy: the Need for Long-Term Policies

A recent IEA publication, *The Power of Transformation*, spells out what can be done. An extremely large share of wind and solar PV, about 45% in annual generation, brings only 10 to 15% higher total costs in the long run. Yet that requires changing approach. Renewables deployment needs to be aligned with overall system development, and the value that renewables bring to the system must be maximized. The remaining system needs to adapt as well, potentially posing a major disparity between the fossil fuel reality in established markets today, and long term ambitions for a cleaner energy system. In stable power markets where demand is stagnating, new generation can only enter the market at the expense of established players, posing political challenges. Still, given the choice, inflexible and polluting assets should make way, rather than keeping cleaner generation sitting idle. In short, integrating renewables smartly can be affordable, and it can be part of the solution to addressing high long-term energy costs, not part of the problem

Whether in stable or dynamic systems, however, barriers to investor confidence must be overcome to secure the particularly high need for capital. Overall, policy uncertainty represents the largest of those barriers. Many renewables no longer require high economic incentives, but they do need long-term policies that continue to provide a predictable and reliable market and regulatory framework compatible with societal goals. For mature renewable electricity markets and technologies, the challenge is for governments to maintain deployment momentum while optimising support costs and maximising benefits to consumers and society; and to enable the system integration of higher shares of variable renewables such as wind power and photovoltaics. For less developed markets and technologies, strategies should focus on stimulating early-stage deployment.

The Cooperation Imperative

In sum, the unconventional revolution in the oil and gas sector is only one part of a changing energy map. Yet those changes will be critical to achieving energy security by meeting growing demand. At the same time, changing patterns can also affect relative competitiveness and market development. Efficient and interconnected markets will be key to addressing price differentials, but energy efficiency will be crucial to maintaining competitiveness in a world of high and variable energy prices. It is efficiency, whether in the form of reduced demand, more efficient plants, or proper price signals, that will also play the principal role in achieving a sustainable energy system.

Major changes are emerging in the energy world in response to shifts in economic growth, efforts at decarbonisation and technological breakthroughs. For decision makers trying to reconcile economic, energy security and environmental objectives, it is essential to be aware of the dynamics at the heart of today's energy market. We have the tools to deal with such profound market change.

Facing common economic and environmental challenges will require international energy cooperation at the highest level, as well as strong mandates for international energy governance structures. The IEA is at the centre of global energy policy, with a core mission to guarantee international energy security while contributing to sustainability and economic prosperity—but to maintain that position it needs to reach beyond its traditional membership. It is for that reason that we are in discussions to further deepen ties with leading non-IEA member energy economies.

CHRISTOPH FREI

Since joining the World Energy Council (WEC) in 2009, Christoph Frei's priorities have been to mobilise international energy leaders and decision-makers to work together towards building a sustainable future, underpinned by robust policymaking. His main focus has been to provide decision-makers with the necessary evidence base and the high-level dialogue platform for energy policies to address the 'energy trilemma'—the trade-offs between energy security, energy equity, and environmental sustainability.

TOWARD A SUSTAINABLE ENERGY FUTURE

As the World Energy Council (WEC) celebrates its 90 years history and the International Forum of the Americas marks its 20th anniversary, the world is experiencing a time of unprecedented uncertainty for the energy sector. Secure, reliable, affordable, clean and equitable energy supply is fundamental to global economic growth and human development and presents huge challenges for us all. Energy demand will continue to increase, driven by non-OECD economic growth. Billions of people still do not have access to electricity and / or clean cooking facilities. The pressing need and the challenges to transform the energy system come at a time when many governments are struggling with significant debt burden and the lingering effects of the global recession. Maintaining a balance between the three legs of the energy trilemma can seem impossible. To make things more daunting, it is in the context of this uncertainty that today's policymakers and business leaders have to take critical decisions on our future energy infrastructure and the use of our world's natural resources to deliver sustainable development.

We can see from our latest World Energy Scenarios report which sets out two worlds (the more consumer-driven Jazz scenario and the more voter-driven Symphony scenario), that demand is going to continue to grow for energy and energy services. Our analysis shows that total primary energy supply is set to increase to 2050 by between 27% and 61%, with fossil fuels remaining the dominant energy source supplying between 59% and 77% of the global primary energy mix. However, electricity generation from renewable energy sources will increase around four to five times by 2050 in comparison to 2010, with solar PV showing the highest increase of approximately 230 times. Currently solar power only accounts for just over 34 TWh/y in the electricity generation mix, but it could provide somewhere between 2,980 TWh and 7,740 TWh in 2050. This equates to between US$2,950 billion and US$9,660 billion of investment in solar, representing the largest potential investment area of any renewable energy resource. At the same time, the development of shale gas in North America has created great uncertainty with the impacts and opportunities for other countries still to play out fully. This is not just in relation to supply of gas but there are also the cause and effects for other technologies. For example, we now see the use of coal increasing utilised in Europe, in contradiction to political will, due in part to cheap displaced resources seeking new markets.[1]

In the past there was only one major signal that energy leaders and policymakers needed to worry about—the price of oil. Now the diversity of the energy mix and rapidly maturing new technologies place significant strain on what has traditionally been a highly conservative sector. Added to this a multiplicity of policy initiatives, the fragmentation of the value chain, and a lack of political clarity in some regions is creating a high level of uncertainty, which if not addressed could lead to significant issues for the global economy.

Over the last five years we have seen the acceleration and increased complexity of energy drivers as well as policy and investment signals. To provide better understanding of the factors behind this

1 World Energy Council, 2013: *World Energy Scenarios—Composing energy futures to 2050*.

increased uncertainty the WEC monitors the issues concerning our energy leaders' community. Today, the primary global issues that keep energy leaders awake and active are[2]:

- Energy prices, and high associated volatility, have become the most critical uncertainty for energy leaders for the first time this year, surpassing the global climate framework.
- The lack of global agreement on climate change mitigation remains a key issue, for the fifth consecutive year, without a clear path for the future of CO_2 prices.
- Access to capital has an increased uncertainty this year, demonstrating the difficulties in the matching of capital with the necessary demand for energy infrastructure.
- Carbon capture, utilisation and storage (CCUS) is perceived with rapidly diminishing impact, continuing the clear trend of the past three years and reinforcing the reality check needed around our ability to deliver on climate objectives by 2050.
- Energy efficiency remains stable in its positioning as an action priority for the fifth successive year and continues to present an immediate opportunity, but will only be realised with a longer-term approach to financing.

It is with the consideration of such outlined complexity and uncertainty that the WEC promotes the energy trilemma approach with the objective to deliver balanced, predictable and stable policy and regulatory frameworks. It is such balance that mitigates political risk, which too often keeps the necessary investments from flowing. I am pleased to report that the energy trilemma as a concept is being recognised by ministers and policymakers across the globe with public endorsements coming from the President of Korea at our recent World Energy Congress. Energy Ministers are incorporating the energy trilemma recommendations into their national energy policies and they are engaging with WEC as a neutral platform to help define a sustainable energy strategy.

---

2 World Energy Council, 2014: *World Energy Issues Monitor - What keeps energy leaders awake at night?*

> "The Trilemma report demonstrates that a sustainable energy future is possible if all of these tools are deployed quickly and at scale."
>
> Christiana Figueres, Executive Director of the United Nation Framework Convention on Climate Change.

We are also seeing industry and investors looking to our supporting Energy Sustainability Index to better assess and manage risk exposure. This tool ranks 129 countries' energy and climate policies.

Driving Sustainable Energy Development

Predictable and durable energy policies that go beyond the political cycle and have clearly defined goals are the cornerstones of a sustainable energy system. To support the formulation of policies, the energy industry needs to be proactive in sharing knowledge and taking a strong role in change management with regards to energy use. Policymakers must ensure that energy policies are: integrated with adjacent policy areas (for example, environment, industry, and transportation); include the promotion and support of energy efficiency; and are generally supported by citizens.

Against this policy backdrop, there is a need to implement consistent, predictable regulatory and legal frameworks to support long-term investment in energy infrastructure. These include the effective use of market-based economic instruments to level the playing field for all energy technologies. Alongside this, there is a role for carefully selected mechanisms to correct market failures such as, 'green' or infrastructure banks, green bonds, well-designed public-private partnerships, and carefully applied subsidies where necessary.

Lastly, public and private initiatives that enable innovation as well as research, development and demonstration (RD&D) projects are necessary to transform the way energy is produced and used. Industry must lead the way in bringing forward technological innovations.[3]

---

3 World Energy Council, 2012: *World Energy Trilemma: Time to get real – The case for sustainable energy policy.*

Future Energy Needs

investment of US$37 trillion (oil and gas supply r US$19 trillion and the power sector, including generation, transmission and distribution accounts for US$17 trillion) is needed in the world's energy supply system over 2012–2035.[4] The majority of the investment (61%) is needed in non-OECD countries. Cash-strapped governments have limited capacity to fund the increased energy access and shift to a low-carbon future. Private sector capital must be attracted to invest in the sector. But, unless investors have a specific mandate to invest in energy projects, the energy sector is facing a competition for capital with other infrastructure projects. The returns on energy investments must be commensurate with levels of risk and also competitive with the returns on other options for investments.

Energy investments require large amounts of long-term, reasonably priced debt and equity finance to provide investors with the necessary returns and ensure affordable energy to consumers. Traditional sources of private finance (debt and equity) for infrastructure projects are becoming more constrained in their capacity to provide long-term capital. Utilities face uncertain energy demand, increased borrowing costs and the need to reduce their leverage to protect their credit ratings. Thus, the commercial market is constrained by risk aversion and a competition for funding resources at banks. The banks, in turn, face capital and liquidity constraints, including legislation requirements for higher capital ratios, and show lesser interest in lending for investments in potentially risky energy projects.

New technologies, particularly new low- or zero-carbon infrastructure and technologies face even greater difficulties in raising capital to demonstrate commercial viability. Private equity, venture funds or infrastructure funds can be sources of investments into energy infrastructure. However, these funds require greater certainty about the legislation governing the returns generated by these projects and more transparency on the funding process and parties involved before they will invest.

---

4 International Energy Agency, 2012: *World Energy Outlook 2012*.

Buttressed against these specific finance challenges is regulatory and political uncertainty that affects large, long-term energy projects and prevents new players to enter the market.

To encourage investments, energy projects must have an attractive risk-return profile to meet the competition for capital. In that context, policymakers and energy leaders called for greater engagement with the financial sector to ensure potential investors have the needed knowledge of the opportunities and risk management mechanisms to support necessary investments in the energy sector.[5]

Financing Development

The challenge is even greater for companies in developing countries, no matter if privately or publicly owned. While policy and regulatory risk are major deterrents to energy investments in general, country risk, for example, expropriation, civil war, and deteriorations in the rule of law, adds an additional layer to an already highly complex situation.

In many instances, the perception of a country's risk can inhibit energy investments even in countries where the underlying economics of the energy sector are strong. In such cases, power companies or projects with very attractive underlying economics cannot secure capital at the right price—even in circumstances where the regulatory processes to build and operate a utility seem similar to those in OECD countries. Differentiating between the sovereign credit of a country and the credit of the power sector of that country, may lead to a very different evaluation result. A sovereign credit rating cap is based on a range of factors within the country profile and economy, only some of which will affect the power sector. Yet in many instances, the economics and attractiveness of energy projects are negatively skewed by a reliance on the sovereign credit rating in assessing the investment. Moving beyond country ratings to support a deeper understanding of energy project economics will be key to unlocking investment especially in developing economies. In that context, the WEC's energy trilemma provides a valuable tool to benchmark a coun-

---

5 World Energy Council, 2013: *World Energy Trilemma: Time to get real – The agenda for change.*

try's political and regulatory risk, which from an investor's perspective is fundamental. It indicates where a lack of balance amongst the three dimensions – energy security, energy equity and environmental sustainability – may expose a country to a risk of push for change of its energy policy, a major deterrent to investment."[6]

Beyond securing funding be it from traditional or non-traditional investors, projects require expertise to support processes such as the preparation of a feasibility study or transactions skills, the lack of which can easily add 2-3 years to the project development process. The lack of effectively scoped energy projects and thereby the non-existence of a project pipeline oftentimes leads to a "crowding-out" of potential investors.

Time to get Real

With the urgency to take critical decisions, more than ever we need an impartial, inclusive and fact-based dialogue on our future. We need to improve our common understanding of the implications of today's decisions and actions so we can make them the ones that deliver the future we want. A key foundation for policy and investment decisions is a thorough understanding of critical drivers and uncertainties, which will define our future and make our energy systems more resilient. The World Energy Council's Scenarios to 2050 in that context provide a set of plausible and coherent stories of how the future may unfold, based on a systemic analysis of critical drivers and uncertainties. They offer a reference point against which to strengthen the foundation for our capacity to define balanced policies, overcome the challenges the energy trilemma presents and take informed investment decisions.

Organisations with a proven track record—the 20 years of the International Economic Forum of the America or the 90 years of the World Energy Council—have an important role to play in supporting intergovernmental processes. However, we are starting to see signs that the world may not be able to wait too much longer. Now is the time to get real in setting out a path for a sustainable energy future.

---

6 World Energy Council, 2013: *2013 Energy Sustainability Index.*

GÉRARD MESTRALLET

Gérard Mestrallet is Chairman and Chief Executive Officer of GDF SUEZ, and graduated from Ecole Polytechnique and Ecole Nationale d'Administration. He joined Compagnie Financière de Suez in 1984 as an advisor to the Chairman. Two years later, he was appointed Executive Vice-President for industrial affairs. In 1991, Mr. Mestrallet was appointed Executive Director and Chairman of the Management Committee of Société Générale de Belgique. In 1995, he became Chairman and Chief Executive Officer of Compagnie de Suez. When Suez merged with Gaz de France, in 2008, he became Chairman and Chief Executive Officer of GDF SUEZ. He is also Chairman of Paris EUROPLACE.

NATURAL GAS: A WINNING SOLUTION

Gil Rémillard, with the support of Paul Desmarais, created the International Economic Forum of the Americas—Conference of Montreal 20 years ago to heighten knowledge of the major issues of economic globalization, on the intuition that our world was about to see some big changes.

Twenty years ago, our Group set itself the goal of becoming one of the global energy leaders, based on three observations: Europe was changing the scale and structure of a sector which had long been nationalized and monopolistic, increasing needs and growth were creating tremendous international development opportunities, and sustainable development was calling for responsible growth.

In the 21st century, the energy industry will undergo tremendous changes that will reshape its landscape. On the gas market in particular we are starting to see signs of a global economy that is moving at three different speeds.

North America is experiencing a genuine revolution that is transforming its economic and energy landscape with the rapid expansion of unconventional gas and oil. Currently, 90% of the world's unconventional gas production is American.[1] The United States has become the leading global gas producer, and unconventional gas could represent half of the country's gas production by 2020. Canada has also started producing unconventional gas. However, although it has comparable resources to the United States,[1] its unconventional gas production is still significantly lower than its neighbour's.

By allowing the United States to become virtually energy independent, unconventional gas has had a significant impact on the American economy, starting with the electrical production sector. Gas power plants made up 39% of the United States' electrical capacity in 2011, up from 25% in 2000.[1] Gas is gradually displacing other fossil fuels to the point where it is dramatically changing transportation. By 2015, one third of the American heavy duty truck fleet could turn to using natural gas.[2]

In broader terms, American industry has gained in competitiveness, increasing national growth and employment opportunities. The rapid expansion of unconventional gas is estimated to have generated 600,000 jobs in the United States, a statistic that could rise to 1.6 million by 2035.[3]

Another direct consequence of the increasing share of gas in the electrical mix is a significant decrease in CO_2 emissions. While the United States has not signed the Kyoto Protocol, it has managed to reduce the energy sector's CO_2 emissions by 13% since 2006, by partially replacing coalfired power plants with gas-powered thermal generation plants.[4]

---

1 Enerdata.
2 CITI Group.
3 IHS CERA Alert.
4 Enerdata.

We are continuing to evaluate the scope of this revolution on an economic, geopolitical and environmental level on a daily basis. It will take a new turn as soon as the United States begins exporting its natural gas by accelerating the globalization of gas markets. Twenty liquefied natural gas (LNG) terminal projects are currently under review in the United States. GDF SUEZ took a very clear position on this issue by taking part in the Cameron project in Louisiana, the sixth LNG terminal project since 2011 to obtain the rights to export its production. GDF SUEZ will participate in the development of natural gas in emerging countries.

Emerging countries have an incredible thirst for energy to ensure their industrial development and provide their populations with access to different energy uses. The energy demand per person will increase by 40% in China and by 150% in India by 2035. Consequently, in the decades to come, non-OECD countries will be the ones driving energy demand. They represent 93% of the increase in energy demand and will represent more than 80% of the additional gas demand[5] between 2011 and 2035.

We will need all of our energy sources to meet this enormous need. Natural gas, however, will see the highest increase in demand from emerging countries by 2035, ahead of coal. It will make up more than a quarter of the new energy demand. Natural gas is in fact doing more than just supporting the economic growth of emerging countries—its share is increasing in the energy mix. It will go from 20% to 22% in non-OECD areas. The development of unconventional gas resources in emerging countries could accelerate this trend, especially in China.

China's five-year plan puts great emphasis on natural gas development. The excessive share of coal in the energy mix—close to 70% of the primary mix—is understandably raising environmental concerns. Furthermore, China is very dependent on oil imports. It has substantial conventional gas resources—the equivalent of 20 years of the current domestic consumption—and 10 times more technically recoverable unconventional gas resources. Natural gas is therefore an obvious national choice, and this was demonstrated by the 15% price increase decided by authorities in July 2013. This policy could quadruple Chinese gas consumption by 2030,

5 IEA, WEO 2013, Scenario New Policies.

potentially increasing the Chinese market to the European market's current size. Of course, in China and other emerging countries, infrastructure remains a major challenge.

For GDF SUEZ, supporting energy development in emerging countries is a strategic priority. Regarding natural gas, we have made a LNG floating storage regasification unit available and will be applying our expertise to the development of underground gas storage in China. We are currently operating an LNG terminal in Chile and building another one in Uruguay. We have made a major shift in our LNG portfolio towards the Pacific Basin.

In Europe, the landscape is radically different. The energy policy has failed on three levels: environment, economy, and security of supply.

Environmentally-speaking, the coal displaced by American shale gas is now pouring into European markets and displacing European gas, causing an increase in CO_2 emissions that has been limited only by the economic crisis. At the same time, European consumers—companies and households—are paying a lot more for energy than those in the United States.

Security of supply is threatened by the closure of gas power plants, which are no longer competitive due in part to renewable energy policies that are disconnected from technology maturity levels and market needs, and the inefficiency of the CO_2 market. According to Capgemini, 130 GW of Europe's capacity is not recovering its fixed costs, out of a European total of 970 GW.

Europe does, however, have significant unconventional gas and oil resources, especially in France and Poland, although it is hesitant to exploit them. This could create a serious rupture in its energy market. GDF SUEZ sees an opportunity for the European economy whereby technological advances could allow for secure, environmentally safe production with limited impact in terms of pollution and ecological footprint.

Diverging Prices in Three Leading Regional Markets

In the United States, gas prices are dropping as a result of increased shale gas production ($3 to $6/MBtu).[6] Prices are higher in Europe ($8 to $12/MBtu), where a liquid market exists alongside partial indexing of long-term contracts on oil prices. The share of volumes traded at market price is growing. Today it represents almost half of the total volume of European gas. In Asia, gas prices have gone even higher ($14 to $16/MBtu) as demand has increased significantly since the Fukushima disaster and the closure of Japanese nuclear power plants. The markets are indexed to the price of oil.

On an international level, the development of marketplaces and the stop-gap role played by LNG is pushing up gas prices, independent of oil prices. This has created a divergence in the prices of these two commodities.

Meeting a Triple Imperative: The Benefits of Natural Gas

• *Security of supply*

The development of unconventional gas has caused the volume of gas production to skyrocket over the last decade, completely disrupting global outlooks. The most recent estimates of the International Energy Association (IEA) show that the world's reserves—of which more than half is unconventional gas—could last for close to 240 years at the current rate.

Of all the fossil fuels, gas is the most evenly distributed geographically, and its economic benefits combined with the prospect of greater energy independence are pushing more and more countries to explore their underground gas reserves. Since 2000, gas production has grown by 38%, at an average rate of 2.7% per year, especially in the Middle East, Asia, Africa and the Commonwealth of Independent States (CIS). Unconventional gas has also brought forward new major players, such as Australia. This country boasts as many unconventional resources as the United States, and is currently developing an integrated gas chain (CBM-to-LNG projects),[7] and could take Qatar's place as the leading exporter of

---

6 MBtu: Million British thermal units (1,000 Mbtu = 22.5 tonnes of oil equivalent).

7 Coal-bed methane or coal gas (unconventional) production and gas liquefaction on the same site.

LNG by 2020. Australian gas will speed up the development of LNG trade in regions across the world, starting with Asia.

By following in North America's footsteps, other countries could benefit from these new resources to increase security and diversity of supply, even though the North American model is not exactly transferrable. This is because North America's geological, industrial, cultural and economic context is particularly favourable to its growth.

Another factor of security of supply is increased trade in natural gas. Developments in transportation infrastructure have allowed market liquidity to increase. One example is the Nord Stream pipeline—9%-owned by GDF SUEZ—which directly connects Russia and Germany. In the last decade, the LNG market has seen tremendous growth marked by an average increase of close to 7% per year. In 2011, LNG represented 31% of international gas trade. By 2030, the LNG market could more than double, growing by more than 4% per year. This strong growth will primarily be led by Asia Pacific. GDF SUEZ is the third largest LNG importer in the world. This is a key driver in our development strategy, especially in Asia, with its strong growth prospects and new supply potential.

• *Competitiveness*

Energy policies need to be sustainable from an economic point of view as energy prices directly impact industry competitiveness and household buying power.

The expansion of renewable energy sources still requiring direct or indirect funding will therefore be gradual. The right balance must be found between market design integration and growth on the learning curve, in order to drive down production costs. Natural gas is an excellent, competitive and flexible complement to electrical production.

Natural gas is also competitive in the residential, industrial and transportation sectors. It increases the competitiveness of the economy as a whole. This is particularly evident in the United States, as we saw earlier.

• *Sustainability*

What is the best energy mix for a world with growing energy needs? One that is balanced, well diversified, and low on carbon emissions. Renewable energy will play a determining role here. Canada is one of the world leaders in this field, with more than half of its electricity produced by hydropower. Renewable energy is being called upon to occupy a growing share of the energy mix in regions across the world. Its share of the world's primary energy consumption will increase from 13% to 18% between 2011 and 2035. Two thirds of this increase will take place in non-OECD countries.[8]

Natural gas also helps reduce the effects of global warming. With half as many CO_2 emissions as coal, and more flexibility, it is an optimal fossil fuel solution. The replacement of coal with gas, and to a lesser extent, oil, has significantly decreased CO_2 emissions in the energy sector. The development of new uses, such as gas marine and motor vehicle fuel, or small-scale LNG, will speed up the shift towards using more substitutes.

In a world where intermittent renewables such as wind and solar are playing an ever-increasing role, there is a growing need for alternative sources to compensate for days without wind or sun. Gas power plants should step in and fill this role. Natural gas is an efficient energy carrier as it can be used in conjunction with particularly advanced equipment, especially for heating: fuel cells, heat pumps, etc.

Natural gas is also a renewable energy carrier thanks to technological advances such as bio gas and power to gas. Bio gas, produced from biomass and garbage, is a key part of the circular economy. It can be injected into existing infrastructures or used as fuel for vehicles. Power-to-gas technology uses the inevitable surplus from renewable electricity to produce hydrogen from water through electrolysis. Hydrogen is now recovered once it is injected into the gas network. In the future, it will be used to produce synthetic methane when combined with CO_2. This is a clever way to store and transport energy while using existing infrastructure.

---

8 IEA, WEO 2013, Scenario New Policies.

GLOBAL ECONOMY

Natural gas is a key part of the 21st century's energy mix. It has huge potential throughout the world, but its growth depends on our industries' capacity to innovate. Innovation will allow us to create and develop new uses, exploit the vast unconventional gas resources available across the globe while complying with the strictest environmental requirements, and build tomorrow's energy markets on which all global economies depend.

MANUFACTURING SECTORS

DOMINIC BARTON

Dominic Barton is Global Managing Director of McKinsey & Company. In his 28 years with the firm, he has served as McKinsey's Asia Chairman from 2004 to 2009 and led the Korea office from 2000 to 2004. Dominic is an active participant in international fora including Davos, the St. Petersburg International Economic Forum, and the Asia Business Council. He has authored more than 80 articles and two books on the role of business in society, leadership, Asia, and the challenges and opportunities facing markets worldwide.

MANUFACTURING: A PROMISING SECTOR

In a time when sleek digital technologies dominate entrepreneurial ambitions and the popular imagination, manufacturing sometimes seems like an old-economy dinosaur. This view, however, couldn't be further from reality. Recent advances in materials, machines, production processes and operations are enabling manufacturers to create entirely new kinds of products and reinvent existing ones. Meanwhile, a massive shift in demand for consumer goods is about to create a manufacturing boom in many industries and regions. Over the next 15 years, 1.8 billion people, mainly from the developing world, will enter the consuming class, nearly doubling global spending and turning their countries from mere links on manufacturing supply chains into critical markets for the end products.

Today, we are poised to enter an era of truly global manufacturing opportunities. When the term "offshoring" was first popularized in the 1990s, it was shorthand for taking advantage of lower wages in developing nations. But it represented much more than that: a decisive change in globalization, made possible by a wave of liberalization in countries such as China and India, and rising skill levels among emerging-market workers, among other factors. Something of equal moment is occurring today. As wages and purchasing power rise in emerging markets, those markets' relative importance as centers of demand, not just supply, is growing. Simultaneously, global energy dynamics are expanding manufacturers' strategic options, while advances stemming from the so-called Internet of Things and other technologies are opening doors to huge operational efficiencies.

Rather than focus on offshoring or even "reshoring"—a term denoting the move of manufacturing back to the developed world as labor costs rise overseas—manufacturers need to concentrate on where their future lies. My colleague Katy George, who co-leads the manufacturing group at McKinsey & Co., refers to this perspective as next-shoring: an approach that emphasizes proximity to demand and proximity to innovation. Both are crucial in a global economy where fast-changing demand patterns reward those who can quickly adapt products to regional tastes, and where suppliers armed with disruptive technologies can bring major competitive advantages. Flexibility, agility and ability to customize on a mass scale will distinguish the manufacturing leaders from the also-rans.

Next-shoring is still taking shape and no doubt will evolve in unexpected ways. What's increasingly clear, though, is that it will radically reshape manufacturing strategies around the world.

Next... Drivers of Demand

Drivers of demand need for a next-shoring mindset is largely rooted in one staggering shift: within a decade, 66% of global demand will come from emerging markets, up from 40% in 2008.

Since more than two-thirds of global manufacturing today occurs in industries that tend to locate close to demand, the impact of this growth will be dramatic.

Regional demand is particularly important in sectors such as automobiles, machinery, food and beverages, and fabricated metals. In the United States, about 85% of the industrial rebound since the financial crisis was due to car and machine production, along with those sectors' regional supplier industries. In China, locally oriented manufacturers have been major contributors to the rising investment and employment. As OEMs expand in emerging markets to serve regional demand, their suppliers follow. The number of automotive-supplier plants in Asia, for example, has tripled in just the past decade.

Along with growth, demand in developing markets is undergoing a rapid fragmentation into numerous product varieties, feature and quality levels, price points, service needs, and marketing channels. The regional, ethnic, income, and cultural diversity of Africa, Brazil, China, and India (where some local segments exceed the size of entire markets in the developed world) is recalibrating what it means to satisfy local preferences. To again use the automobile example, the splintering of demand in that sector has led to a 30 to 50% increase in the number of vehicle models.

The surging appetite for consumer goods in developing economies helps explain why rapid wage growth in China hasn't choked off manufacturing expansion there. Wages have nearly doubled since 2008, partly as a result of domestic minimum-wage policies. In a few trade-oriented industries, such as apparel production and consumer electronics, lower labor costs still tend to dictate where manufacturers locate. But just as Henry Ford's $5 payday helped create a new consuming class, so higher wages in China are increasing local spending, thus reinforcing manufacturers' local-investment choices.

Dropping energy costs are another factor influencing location decisions. The price of natural gas in the United States has fallen by two-thirds as gas production from shale deposits has risen. While sectors such as petrochemicals, fertilizer, and steel are benefiting from these declines, this doesn't necessary presage a major rebalancing of global manufacturing activity. Electricity costs were already lower in the United States than in many countries. And fossil fuels aren't the only area where the energy-supply picture is morphing. Energy-storage technologies, such as lithium-ion batteries and fuel cells, are becoming more powerful and less costly. At the same time, the growing affordability of renewable energy—particularly solar and wind power—offers manufacturers an expanding range of supply options. As advances continue, more and more companies will be able to treat the availability and price of energy as lesser concerns in their strategic bets—leading them back to a focus on local demand patterns.

Next...Technology Innovations

Technological advances are driving far more than energy dynamics. Innovations in robotics, 3-D printing and digital operations promise to fundamentally reshape how companies plan their manufacturing costs and footprints.

Robotics: Investments in industrial robots have increased by nearly 50% since 2008, producing a new generation of robotic systems with greater dexterity and data-processing ability. These robots can perform an expanding array of factory tasks, ranging from manipulating small electronic parts to picking and packing products. They can work side by side with humans and be trained by factory-floor operators rather than programmed by highly paid engineers. By lowering companies' reliance on human labor, such robots are yet another reason manufacturers may locate close to demand centers, even where wage rates are relatively high. In developing nations, robots could speed up rates of automation and help bridge shortages of some production skills. Our research suggests that up 25% of industrial workers' tasks in developed countries, and up to 15% of those in developing countries, could be automated by 2025.

3-D printing: This technology has the potential to be truly transformative. While 3-D printers today comprise only a sliver of value in the manufacturing sector (0.02%), their sales are set to double by 2015, and prices are declining swiftly. Such printers open up the possibility of more distributed production networks and radical customization. Companies are already using these devices for making prototypes in-house, accelerating product development. In time, 3-D printing will enable manufacturers to replace some parts suppliers with in-house printers. For some specialized goods, it's easy to foresee the emergence of service businesses—the equivalent of print shops—that would manufacture items based on design specifications provided by B2B or B2C customers.

Digitized operations: Robotics and 3-D printers are only parts of a much bigger shift transforming the factory floor. Cloud computing, mobile communications, and the Internet of Things are beginning to combine with analytics to create threads of intelligent data that link plants, managers and buyers as never before. Increasingly, products will communicate with each other, with robots and other machines inside factories, and with customers and suppliers. Such digitization of operations will enable companies to get a clear view of who makes what, where—and how well. Executives will be able to run virtual operations "war rooms" on their phones, solving plant-floor optimization problems remotely as intelligent machines interact with each other and with people on the line. Crowdsourced design and on-demand production will allow manufacturers to sell previously underutilized lines by the hour as they rely on dynamic databases to determine what every part should cost.

Sound like a futuristic fantasy? Consider this: GE already has a 400-person industrial Internet software team and its employees use iPads to run an advanced battery factory in New York State. Amazon is employing growing numbers of smart warehouse robots. One auto supplier recently slashed an eight-month prototyping process to one week.

Next...Manufacturing Paradigm

Although these technological and economic forces are still gathering strength, they point to two defining priorities for manufacturers in advanced and emerging markets alike: being close to demand, and investing in innovation (particularly in supplier choices). Next-shoring isn't about manufacturing moving from one place to another but about companies adapting to, and preparing for, the changes in their sector and making decisions accordingly.

Where to locate: At a time when growing demand in emerging markets is multiplying regional product preferences, being close to customers is particularly important. In a 2012 interview with McKinsey, Timken CEO James Griffith explained that over the previous ten years, the company strongly expanded its Eastern European, Indian, and Chinese manufacturing. Why? Not because wages are low there, "but because those were the markets that were growing," he told us. This expansion has been accompanied by a strategic shift away from automotive parts and toward meeting the needs of emerging-market customers in mining, trucking, steelmaking, and cement-making.

As new products, market segments, and consumer preferences combine with perennial risks, such as seasonal variations in demand, uncertainty in the industry is growing. That uncertainty, in turn, puts a premium on operational agility—the ability to adapt design, production, and supply chains rapidly to fluctuating conditions—and makes location decisions all the more important. Take the experience of a consumer-products company that had relied on one plant to supply its major market. When the company began experiencing unaccustomed spikes in regional and seasonal purchasing patterns, shortages ensued. To accommodate this rising variability, the company built a second, similar plant in a different region. The additional capacity helped ensure supplies to the prime market while allowing the firm to opportunistically respond to growing demand in several markets close to the new plant. The investment was considerable, but it lowered the manufacturer's risk exposure, eliminated lost sales, and improved the bottom line.

Which suppliers to use: As technical expertise and knowledge of local markets increasingly shape product strategies, responsive and tech-savvy supplier networks will be vital factors in battles for regional dominance. One major manufacturer seeking to exploit new technology decided to shift from a low-cost parts supplier in Mexico to one with cutting-edge 3-D printing capabilities. The new relationship has lowered stocking costs (since parts are made on demand), while opening the door to faster prototyping.

Examples like this are just a start. As manufacturing partners invest in more collaboration, they will gain benefits ranging from more reliable logistics to better payment systems. First, though, manufacturers will need to make significant upgrades to their supplier bases, jointly improving their capabilities in areas like robotics. Management investment in skill-development programs may be necessary as well. In some cases, manufacturers may find it valuable to collaborate with local or national governments to help foster state-of-the-art manufacturing ecosystems.

How to train people: Advances in manufacturing will place a premium on skilled staff, creating a range of regional challenges. In Europe and the United States, educational institutions aren't producing enough workers with the technical skills manufacturers need. In developing economies, the millions of workers well adapted to routine manufacturing may find it difficult to climb to the next level without more training. Line supervisors—often fresh out of regional universities—struggle to manage more complex operations. Companies will need to boost investment in formal training and on-the-job coaching, and support local community colleges and technical institutes in order to shape curricula and gain access to new talent.

A related challenge is the need for more sophisticated management. As manufacturers find it harder to compete based on labor costs, regional managers will need to become both more versatile and better at running a tight operational ship. They'll need to grasp the productivity potential of a range of new technologies and have enough ground-level market knowledge to influence product strategies and investment trade-offs. The ability to build external relationships—with suppliers, education partners, and local-government officials—will also provide a competitive advantage.

The new manufacturing era will challenge many players but it will produce significant benefits for entire economies. The industry's future leaders will be highly agile, networked enterprises that use information and analytics as skillfully as they employ talent and machinery to deliver products and services to diverse global markets. In advanced markets, manufacturing will continue to drive innovation, exports, and productivity growth. In developing countries, the sector will provide a pathway to higher living standards. As economies mature, manufacturing will become more important for its ability to drive productivity growth, innovation, and trade.

Next-shoring will look different in different locations. Europe and the United States have impressive advantages in areas such as biopharmaceuticals, automotive engineering, and advanced materials. China, meanwhile, is quickly climbing the expertise curve, with increasingly sophisticated research facilities and growing experience in advanced processes and industries. In the world we're entering, the question won't be whether to produce in one market for another but how to find the needed expertise to tailor product strategies for each. Those that fail to adapt to the new conditions risk something worse than shrinking market share. They may well face extinction.

Individual Mass Customization: Consumer choice has grown steadily since the buyers of Henry Ford's Model T could pick any color—as long as it was black. In recent years, companies have been expanding ways in which customers can tailor products to their preferences. Now, technology is making this increasingly viable at scale, ushering in *individual* mass customization—building a unique product for each customer. At McKinsey, we've identified seven technologies that will drive mass customization in manufacturing, either by making it easier to offer genuine benefits for consumers or to control costs for producers.

Social technologies: Social media and crowdsourcing are improving customization by allowing companies to gauge the value consumers attach to various product features. Starbucks' frappuccino.com, for example, lets customers build their own virtual drinks using ingredients such as raspberry flavoring and protein powder. This allows Starbucks to measure the popularity of different ingredients and the appeal of combinations before investing in changes at its stores. By inviting consumers to create real or virtual products, companies can in effect use customers as marketers and co-creators happy to broadcast their creations to their social networks.

Interactive configurators: Online configurators are at the heart of mass customization because they provide a quick, user-friendly way to gather buyer preferences. In the past, offering a wide range of configuration options was cumbersome and expensive for manufacturers, but advances in product visualization and configuration software have transformed the process. Shoes of Prey, for example, is a website that lets shoppers configure custom shoes. Buyers select from general shoe types, then pick designs for the toe, back, heel, and decorations. The company has found that the more sophisticated models of the customized product increased conversion rates online by 50%.

3-D scanning and modeling: New 3-D scanners can analyze the shape of real-world objects and collect data needed for constructing 3-D digital models. These tools make it much easier to measure, for example, a human body for tailored products, and the accuracy of the resulting measurements is often better than that of hand measuring. Several companies already offer scanning software that gathers body measurements, which can then be rendered into personalized 3-D models online. In the future, 3-D scanning and modeling might move directly into the home, giving consumers the ability to scan themselves, upload the 3-D model, and order "tailor-made" clothing.

Recommendation engines: Used for years to drive e-commerce by recommending products based on buyers' previous selections, recommendation engines are now moving into the customization space. Chocri, for example, operates a site called createmychocolate.com that helps consumers configure their own chocolate bars from four base chocolates and 100 different toppings. Chocri estimates that its recommendation engine has increased the rate of conversion by more than 30%.

Dynamic pricing: Custom orders can challenge companies with unpredictable spikes in demand, resulting in long wait times that in turn alienate consumers. Smart algorithms and powerful data processing can help overcome this obstacle by shaping consumer behavior through dynamic pricing. One US pizza chain that lets customers configure their own pizzas found that some ingredients, such as sliced toppings, take longer to place on the pizza base. When there is a large backlog of orders, prices on the website adjust dynamically: algorithms decrease prices for toppings that are quicker to place and increase prices for ones that take longer, discouraging consumers from choosing those.

Enterprise and production software: Traditional technology for enterprise resource planning and supply-chain management (SCM) was designed to handle a limited variety of products. Translating an individual order into a custom picking list and assembly instructions for warehouse and production workers was a big challenge. But companies such as Just in Time Business Consulting and Configure One now offer software that lets manufacturers track discrete design features in orders and translate them into sourcing and production instructions. By connecting the configurators at the front end with the production and SCM systems, such tools not only tell the production staff what to assemble but give customers realistic lead times and progress updates.

Flexible production systems: To make small-batch production profitable, flexible manufacturing is essential. Ford and General Motors already use robotic systems with interchangeable tooling that can switch easily between models. The advent of 3-D printing is taking manufacturing flexibility to a whole new level. These devices can print objects with materials such as ceramics, metals, and even chocolate. While primarily used in prototyping, 3-D printers are making inroads into the mass production of customized objects, such as jewelry. As this technology matures, the primary constraint in its adoption will be the creativity of people applying it.

AVI REICHENTAL

Prior to joining 3D Systems, Avi Reichental, President and Chief Executive Officer of 3D Systems since September 2003, served in various senior executive positions with Sealed Air Corporation. Avi is a passionate maker and community service leader. He is the recipient of the regional 2011 E&Y entrepreneur of the year award, the 2012 Financial Times Boldness in Business award and holds 25 U.S. patents. Avi currently serves as faculty chair of the Digital Fabrication Program at Singularity University and is a member of the XPRIZE innovation board and the NCOHF board also known as America's ToothFairy.

'MANUFACTURING THE FUTURE' WITH 3D

It was near midnight in Valencia, California. The year was 1983. Chuck Hull, a design engineer and part-time inventor, excitedly called his wife Antoinette on the phone, "Hurry, come and see the first 3D printed part." Already in her pajamas, she murmured back, "It better be good." It was better than good. That night, in a tiny basement lab, through a process he called stereolithography, Chuck Hull birthed the world's first three-dimensionally printed object, fundamentally altering the course of design and manufacturing history and forever redefining the 'making of things'.

Breakthrough technologies can precipitate sudden and seismic shifts in the way we think, create and function. In few short decades, a mere blip on the timeline of human technological advancement, the Internet has brought unparalleled connectivity and access to information for billions. Even more recently, social networks have transformed the way we gather news and share experiences, satisfying our previously unarticulated needs to digitally congregate and collaborate.

Yet, despite the obvious impact that these radical innovations have on society, the human condition has a near-boundless capacity to ignore, and even deny, the transformative ideas and technologies hidden in plain sight. It is not until these breakthrough ideas become mainstream that we sit back and marvel, just how, exactly, we were able to exist without them.

We sit at a similar juncture today. Exponential advances in cloud computing, artificial intelligence, smart sensing and robotics have converged to catapult another exponential technology, 3D printing, into the forefront of a new technological paradigm: distributed and localized manufacturing. Until now, 3D printing has remained a relatively obscure technology, its complexity and costs making it practical only for deep-pocketed corporations with specific design and manufacturing needs. Yet even in relative immaturity, 3D printing impacts everything we interact with today, from the cars we drive and airplanes we fly, to the shoes and eyeglasses we wear. However, as 3D printing's capabilities have advanced and price points have dropped, the technology has become a catalyst in a manufacturing renaissance that is already changing the way we design, make and consume.

Two and a half centuries ago, the industrial revolution gave rise to unprecedented gains in human productivity and prosperity. Yet in the process, this revolution eradicated localized manufacturing as we knew it, and atrophied many of the vital craftsmanship tools and artisan skills needed for local sustainability. Production became centralized. Hulking machines and assembly lines depersonalized the art of 'making'. Products became increasingly commoditized, uniform and cheap, but the reduction in price obscured the much greater costs of a polluted planet and diminished worker livelihood. At the same time, rising barriers to entry such as capital expenditure consolidated industrial production to only the largest corporations. As a consequence, product creation and innovation became gated by cost and complexity. The process became so pronounced and so institutionalized, we even gave it a fancy name: design for manufacturing.

3D Printing Opens the Manufacturing Field

Fast forward to 2014 and the manufacturing revolution is now underway. The single greatest benefit of a 3D printer is that complexity, the *de facto* currency of the centralized, industrial era, is free. The printer doesn't care if it prints a simple rudimentary geometry or the most exquisitely complex object; there is neither barrier nor penalty for complexity. Therefore, almost overnight, 3D printing technology has leveled the manufacturing playing field, allowing all participants, large or small, to create and disseminate their ideas and products. The question now is "Where do we go from here?"

For many years, the conventional wisdom surrounding 3D printing suggested that the ability to manufacture millions of one-of-a-kind objects directly from a digital design would usher in the era of just-in-time mass customization. In many cases, this has proven to be the case. Medical device companies, for example, eagerly adopted 3D printers to manufacture bespoke hearing aids, orthodontic aligners and surgical tools for knee and hip replacements by the millions.

The broader trends in the 3D printing industry, however, point to a future that goes well beyond mass customization. Working with companies like Nike, Google and General Motors, all leaders in their respective fields, we are beginning to understand that the ability to manufacture millions of identical yet highly complex parts is the true potential of 3D printing. This application of 3D printing allows us to create 'sustainable functionality' with high performance products that exceed all existing benchmarks for precision and durability, in ways we never thought possible. The implications for industries such as aerospace, automotive and consumer goods are profound and overturn hundreds of years of manufacturing precedent.

So How does it Work?

Referred to as "additive manufacturing" in certain industrial circles, 3D printing defies traditional "subtractive" methods of production (the act of carving a statue out of a marble block, for example) by building the product from the bottom up, one layer at a time. This inverse method results in a more efficient and flexible outcome, as additive manufacturing has unlimited manufacturing path flexibility to create complex shapes. Moreover, while subtractive manufacturing often results in an unusable waste byproduct, additive manufacturing uses only the material required to create the final product.

Significant enhancements in sustainability are not the only advantage of additive manufacturing. Because the printer follows the precise cross-sectional patterns prescribed by the design file, 3D printing offers an unmatched reliability and replicability in manufacturing, regardless of design complexity. This capability opens unimagined doors in engineering. Take, for example, a curving internal cooling channel integrated into overall part design. Whereas traditional subtractive methods limit structural possibilities based on the type, size or path of the tools required, 3D printing voids these limitations. Because 3D printing is an integrated process; there is no change in method to accommodate the specifics of an object. This means there is no added lead-time, overhead tooling costs or set up costs required for complicated objects, customizations or even fully functional assemblies. Because 3D printing lets designers place material precisely where it is needed, designs can be made with built-in structures that make it possible to reduce final part count and weight. These reductions are especially useful in automotive and aerospace applications, as they lead to functional components that are lighter and more fuel-efficient.

Since its inception, a wide array of materials have become available for use with 3D printers, including engineered metals, waxes, rubber-like materials, ceramics, plastics, nylons and new age composites. Increasingly found in all industries, 3D printers have become an indispensable part of the design-to-manufacturing process. They are now even migrating to living rooms, where they provide on-demand housewares and entertainment products for families, and classrooms, where they provide true hands-on immersion for students. A rapidly growing number of parents and educators have found that adopting and providing access to 3D printing equips children with the entrepreneurial and creative skills necessary for tomorrow's workplace. In fact, a 2011 report by the Atlantic Council cites Harvard Press predictions that 3D printing is as close as 5-10 years away from mass adoption.

Mainstreaming 3D printing necessitates the removal of the last remaining skill-, technology- and cost barriers. Thankfully, these changes are already underway as 3D printing companies adopt Moore's Law and compete to create the most capable products at more affordable prices. But that is not enough. The 3D printing sector must be democratized if it is to succeed, giving users in every segment the hardware and software tools necessary to create, consume and share 3D printed products. Here, too, we see great progress. Online communities and marketplaces for the sharing, selling and download of 3D files are flourishing. Gamification content creation is drastically lowering the intimidation factor for the technology and increasing its rate of adoption. And with the arrival of sub-$1000 plug-n-play 3D printers intended for kids and their parents, the number of users in the global 3D printing community continues to grow at a feverish pace.

At the other end of the spectrum, ultra high-end 3D printers serve a multitude of applications that permeate our everyday life. Automotive and aerospace engineers use 3D printing for design verification, as well as prototyping and producing end-use parts. F-18 fighter jets, for example, are manufactured with over ninety 3D printed parts. The F-35 model, currently under development, will have 900. Companies like General Electric are using 3D printers to create a new generation of jet engines designed to reduce fuel burn by at least 1.5%, saving billions of dollars in fuel over the lifetime of an airplane.

Uses for industrial grade 3D printers extend well beyond high-tech machinery. Architectural firms craft complex, full color models in record time. Jewelers create wax molds to instantly cast designs. Manufacturers all over the world, from shoemakers to power tool producers, have embraced 3D printing in their quest to accelerate development cycles.

From custom hearing aids to dental restorations, few sectors have benefited from 3D printing technology more than health care. Customized Invisalign orthodontics aligners, for example, are 3D printed *en masse*, at volumes of over 65,000 unique molds each day. Now personalized prosthetics can be 3D printed, and developments are even underway to 3D print human organs. This breakthrough could significantly reduce the number of transplant rejections by fashioning replacement organs using the recipient's own tissues as the material.

To Revamp our World

As if these extensive and expanding capabilities were not enough, 3D printing carries with it yet another game-changing capability: teleporting physical mass. Because 3D printing enables the movement of buildable designs, real products can be 'virtually faxed' or e-mailed across the globe to a 3D printer near you. One positive result of this functionality is that commonly outsourced items may be re-localized through 3D printing, and inventory costs may be reduced or eliminated, all while shrinking the carbon footprint of global freight.

The ability to print on-demand parts also has security implications, both desirable and undesirable. For the military, 3D printing offers remote locations replenishable access to an entire catalogue of spare tools and parts. Equipping base camps or ships with 3D printers could ease the spatial and material burden of stocked supply closets, while allowing valuable and limited space to be repurposed. On the other hand, in a society that can digitize, teleport and replicate designs with impunity, printable weapons and democratized counterfeiting pose stark new challenges for law enforcement agencies and defense departments around the world. These implications, and the endless array of unexplored uses and new frontiers for 3D printing, are why this technology is considered to be truly "disruptive".

In the first State of the Union address of his second term, President Obama highlighted 3D printing as a technology replete with opportunity, one which may hold the key to reviving the United States' dwindling manufacturing sector. Obama made specific reference to the first hub of the National Additive Manufacturing Innovation Institute (NAMII), which opened in 2012 in Youngstown, Ohio, and announced the launch of more such programs in 2014. According to President Obama, these hubs are intended to be places "where businesses will partner with the Departments of Defense and Energy to turn regions left behind by globalization into global centers of high-tech jobs." Obama plans to create a network of these hubs that will "guarantee that the next revolution in manufacturing is 'Made in America'". The revolution will indeed happen in the United States, but not exclusively. 3D printing has the potential to empower communities all over the world and inject dynamism into any economy. In other words, the next revolution in manufacturing will occur everywhere and with everything, locally and more sustainably.

Some have argued that 3D printing will kill what is left of our manufacturing jobs, when in fact 3D printing may actually provide the greatest democratization of production the world has ever known. By imparting a new kind of literacy that transcends borders and languages, leapfrogging complex tools and bridging virtual and actual, 3D printing has the capacity to completely level the playing field of manufacturing. 3D printing introduces a new age where everyone can become an expert maker. Not only will new jobs arise in advanced manufacturing within 3D printing, but precisely because of 3D printing there will be new opportunities for artists, engineers, educators and entrepreneurs.

Because 3D printing quickly turns virtual designs into physical, functional parts, perhaps the most revolutionary benefit of the technology is its ability to revamp and restyle product development and commercialization, from production to distribution, and every phase in between. This benefit is decentralized and accessible, not only to companies and industries, but to individuals and consumers as well. The portability and sharability of digital design files opens up limitless possibilities for crowdsourcing designs and co-creation that are only now beginning to be explored. Cloud-printing services (the satellite fulfillment and shipment of digitally submitted 3D printing files) are likewise facilitating mass access regardless of mass adoption, translating to substantially lower barriers to entry for manufacturing. Such services enable garage entrepreneurs to bring new concepts to market with never-before-seen ease and speed.

Yet the innovations that address familiar products may prove to be just as imaginative and impactful as those yet to be developed. The 3D printed guitars and basses by New Zealand designer Olaf Diegel, for example, can substitute the exotic and endangered woods used in manufacturing and replace them with more sustainable materials. Diegel's instrument patterns also capture personalities and moods that can be customized to fit the musician in entirely new ways; just one more example of how 3D printing can help us rethink and recast our most time-honored products and processes.

Drastic changes are underway in the kitchen as well, as 3D printing gives bakers, pastry chefs and chocolatiers the ability to conjure delectable structures that have never before been possible. And confections are just the beginning. Working with Dutch researchers from the Netherlands' Organisation for Applied Scientific Research (TNO), 3D Systems is exploring disruptive food creations that could revolutionize personalized nutrition, performance foods and flavorful puréed foods for the elderly. Of course, accessibility is a key component in new product adoption. Since we do not expect chefs and cooks to become CAD-ers and coders, we are simultaneously developing a digital cookbook companion that allows anyone to successfully experiment with the fusion of shapes and ingredients with gamified stylizers. After all, the more participants that join the 3D printing community, the more innovative, more productive, and more creative that community becomes. It is therefore our mission at 3D Systems to democratize this technology.

Sitting in his basement lab 30 years ago, Chuck Hull probably looked down at that first 3D printed part, a small cup, and thought about the future. Yet in a way, his technology has returned us to a more capable version of our pre-industrial past. Through 3D printing, we are reclaiming the power to create. We have married virtual design with physical production and are entering into a bold new era of localized, digital craftsmanship. We are, in a very real sense, going back to basics and honoring the past by manufacturing the future.

CONCLUSION

FIVE FACTORS OF GROWTH TRENDS

The authors of the chapters of this book share a sense of cautious optimism regarding world economic growth. Six years after the Great Recession, we are in a period of recovery, although considerable uncertainty remains.

While the U.S. economy continues to drive this as yet modest global upturn, the European Union has committed to a path towards economic recovery that remains tenuous. This is due in large part to a high unemployment rate, particularly among youth, and the resulting threat of deflation. After 15 years of stagnation, Japan is attempting to reach an inflation target which, however modest, would lend credence to the new policies implemented by Prime Minister Shinzo Abe. Asia is struggling under the influence of China's slowing economy, which is newly focused on its domestic market, but remains bogged down by global competition and tensions with its trading partners.

The emerging BRIC countries (Brazil, Russia, India and China), once the focus of so much hope at the start of globalization, are today facing difficult financial situations that render economic growth more problematic. The threat of recession is looming in Brazil, stemming from the significant devaluation of its currency and the drop in demand for raw materials, particularly in China, among other factors. India is also going through a difficult economic transition, with a devalued currency requiring it to spend more on debt repayment and less on domestic development. Russia's situation has been complicated by the recent economic sanctions imposed further to events in the Ukraine, on top of an existing need to address its debt. To this is added the potential impacts of the energy revolution, which could enable some of its client countries to become less dependent, or even self-sufficient, as they exploit their own sources of oil and shale gas. Africa's economy depends on the raw materials and energy markets, making it particularly vulnerable if demand and prices continue to drop. Meanwhile, major strides in technological development have allowed it to maintain support for a domestic market that is showing strong growth.

Latin America is in a similar situation, although its economy could continue to grow under the influence of an increasingly continental American economy. This could mitigate the effects of the drop in demand from China and revive the movement toward the economic integration of the Americas. In 2001, at the Quebec Conference of the Americas, a broad consensus was reached regarding an integrated continental economy; however, in 2005, a ministerial meet on the topic in Cancun failed. Now, nine years later, Latin America—having returned to democracy except for Cuba—is realizing more and more that it must look to the North for sustainable economic development.

This summary of the world economy leads us to conclude that we are in a new economic cycle that is in some ways the second phase of economic globalization. While the first phase began 20 years ago with economic globalization and led us, through its broad liberalism, to the Great Recession of 2008, this second phase should allow us to make the necessary adjustments to return to a path of global economic growth that is more stable and equitable.

An Adjustment Period

In the wake of the creation of the WTO in 1994, people applauded the end of the nation-state and the regulatory state. Today, we realize that we need to return to a healthy balance through, on the one hand, a liberalism that can encourage investments in job and wealth creation, and, on the other, a state that is more aware of the difficult economic realities requiring it to find new ways to guarantee the quality of public services in a more inclusive society. This has led us to rethink the three main responsibilities of governments to ensure sustainable growth: jobs, investments and technological innovation.

In fact, it is becoming more and more evident that employment is the key indicator of a healthy economy. We must not only examine the overall unemployment rate but also better understand unemployment with regard to the demographic evolution of our societies and the ability of young people to contribute. The youth unemployment rate is particularly high in Europe, which could lead to emigration and then possibly affect the ability of certain countries to develop economically in the future. As for China, it must make adjustments in light of its ageing population, which will number 400 million people over the age of 60 within the next 30 years—one of the consequences of that country's one-child policy.

Job creation is a mixed responsibility belonging to both the state and the private sector. First and foremost, it is the responsibility of businesses to create jobs. However, it is up to our governments to create a supportive economic climate that will encourage businesses to invest. During this period of uncertainty, companies are simply not investing enough. According to a recent study by Deloitte, one third of the world's largest non-financial companies have stockpiled over $2.8 trillion in unspent cash. Meanwhile, governments are still quite limited in their ability to implement investment incentives.

In fact, world debt has increased by 80% since the economic crisis six years ago. Governments are finding themselves in the difficult position of needing to reduce their enormous sovereign debt while continuing to stimulate the economy to support its recovery—not an easy balance to strike. We are aware that governments have very little leeway in this regard; if they do not take steps to significantly reduce their debt, another severe recession, or even depression, could occur.

As a result, governments have little choice but to develop new approaches to encouraging investments and creating jobs, as well as ensuring the quality and accessibility of key public services such as health, education, infrastructure and pensions, with a view to fostering a more inclusive economy. In light of this, Obamacare is a particularly interesting example of a public-private partnership with insurance companies to ensure the quality of a vital public service. This new American health care policy warrants a closer look, as it could serve as a useful model to many governments interested in public-private partnerships.

A New Era of Public-Private Partnerships

The 2008 economic crisis highlighted the need for an alternative governance model to that which prevailed during the 20th century. Things will never return to how they were before 2008. The New Capitalism, which is being referred to more and more, is by necessity founded on the notion of partnership in the truest sense of the word, that is to say, trust.

We are entering into a new era of public-private partnerships, which could allow governments to maintain their capacity to intervene in support of the economy during this period of imposed austerity, while ensuring that private business is there to guarantee the funding and quality of public services through appropriate management under government supervision. Indeed, one of the foundations of this approach is the "user pays" principle. This requires governments to ensure the accessibility of basic services—both physically, meaning that the services are nearby close distance, and materially, meaning that users can afford to pay for them.

Public-private partnerships could be a solution as long as we remember that governments are a different kind of partner, given that their raison d'être is to protect the public interest. Governments can also be a major source of capitalization since, by investing in areas such as technological innovation and research, they have a long-term ability to create a favourable climate for private businesses to create jobs, which is the basis for all sustainable growth.

However, in the context of a global economy, innovation raises the issue of intellectual property rights, for which we have yet to establish universal standards. On the contrary, in the agrifood sector, the issue of intellectual property rights resulted in an impasse at the Doha Round. Yet this remains a critical issue, since the digital revolution combined with the energy revolution is ushering in a third industrial revolution. From advancements in robotics to the advent of 3D printing, and the use of cheaper, more accessible energy sources, the manufacturing sector must redefine itself and rethink its standards of productivity. Moreover, businesses must rethink their competitiveness in light of major new trade routes being put in place.

New International Trade Routes

The free trade agreement signed by Canada and the European Union in 2013 is heralding a new era of international trade taking shape in the Atlantic. Mexico signed a free trade agreement with the European Union several years ago, while the United States is currently involved in negotiations towards such an agreement. Mercosur, which includes Argentina, Uruguay, Venezuela, Bolivia (pending ratification) and Brazil, is also preparing to proceed with formal negotiations regarding its own free trade agreement with the European Union. Thus, in five to seven years, this new trade network, which will also include free trade zones such as NAFTA, should become a new driving force of the global economy. This economy will be fuelled, on the one hand, by a more integrated, stronger European Union, and on the other, by a U.S. economy strengthened by its energy self-sufficiency, as described by Chairman and CEO of GDF SUEZ Gérard Mestrallet in this book.

Another commercial route—the Trans-Pacific Partnership—which currently involves 12 countries, is in development and could be implemented within 7 to 10 years. It could eliminate over $2 trillion in customs tariffs on goods and services traded between the United States, Mexico, Canada, Australia, Brunei, Chile, Japan, Malaysia, New Zealand, Peru, Singapore and Vietnam. These transatlantic and transpacific negotiations will be rounded out by upcoming talks between China and the European Union, as well as with Canada, and, eventually, the United States.

This next generation of free trade agreements will accomplish much more than simply removing trade barriers. In particular, these agreements include regulatory regimes compatible with agreement goals, guarantees for foreign investors, binding provisions regarding the application of intellectual property law, and even labour mobility policies.

Thus, the three foundations of growth, namely employment, investments, and technological innovation, must now exist in relation to one another, each adjusting to their national and international context on an economic, social, cultural and political level. In light of these new free trade agreements, governments will have to strike a balance, over the next 15 years, between austerity and economic development aimed at job creation and guaranteeing access to capital.

Vigilant Central Banks

The asset-backed commercial paper crisis and housing bubble which caused the Great Recession of 2007-2008 taught us that a *laissez-faire* approach can have severe consequences. No one predicted this bubble, which dragged us into the worst recession since the Great Depression of the 1930s.

The question is, are we any better equipped today to identify bubbles before they burst? The answer is in the hands of our central banks, which have played a vital role in supporting economic recovery since 2008. The Federal Reserve has set the tone with its remarkable ability to analyze the situation and take relevant and effective action since the start of the crisis. By continuing in the same vein as her predecessor, Ben Bernanke, Janet Yellen, the new Chair, confirms the Federal Reserve's commitment to limiting easy access to capital, while remaining entirely transparent and strongly connected to the growth of the U.S. economy. This restores confidence in stock markets and investors. Restoring confidence must remain the primary concern for our national and international financial agencies. As Paul Desmarais, Jr. writes in his preface to this work: "Trust in the fairness of the economic system and of public policies will lead citizens to contribute their ingenuity, talents and skills to their nation's economy."

The European Central Bank (ECB) plays a key role in this regard by supporting its countries' economies while maintaining a realistic approach in its demands for balanced budgets. The mistakes made early on to the detriment of the Greek economy are a testament to the importance of securing a fundamental stability that cannot be based on any pre-existing model defined by international experts. Greece and Spain's recent success in selling government bonds demonstrates how the ECB, by working closely with its countries, has been able to restore investor confidence.

In addition, as emphasized in the article by Christian Noyer, Governor of the Bank of France, the European Union has managed to stabilize aspects of its financial system, which also inspires confidence. Under the leadership of Commissioner Michel Barnier, Europe's new banking regulations provide the backbone for this growth, as they are among the strictest in the world. Combined with Basel III, these regulations give the European Union a financial system that is both well integrated and effective in guaranteeing sustainable growth and counteracting the threat of deflation.

Towards a More Modest Growth Era Due to Five Factors

Through their expertise, the contributors to this book have made it clear that the process of economic recovery is well underway. However, we are facing the prospect of a new growth era that is very different from anything we knew prior to the 2008 crisis. We can identify five key factors that will have a major impact on its evolution:

1. Governments' need to achieve financial stability by striking a balance between paying off their sovereign debt and stimulating the economy by creating jobs and by reducing the excessive gap between rich and poor, while continuing to foster investor and consumer confidence.
2. The digital revolution, along with robotics and 3D printing in particular, and their impact on the productivity and competitiveness of businesses, which are adapting to a third industrial revolution, as well as new transatlantic, transpacific and Asian trade routes.
3. The energy revolution, with the increasing exploitation of oil and shale gas reserves and other alternative production methods, which will allow the United States and a number of other countries to become not only self-sufficient but also exporters in the near future.
4. The communication revolution, which has allowed us to access and share information instantly, including the increasingly important impact of social media on the entire world, without requiring any major infrastructure.
5. The need to respect the limits to sustainable development imposed by the increasingly problematic effects of global warming, for a planet that will number more than 9.6 billion inhabitants between now and 2050, according to the United Nations.

The real impact that these factors may have on the growth of the global economy is hard to predict, since they must be understood in relation to: the value of currency, which is always subject to international speculation or manipulation through protectionist measures by the United States; demographic impacts, in the case of a number of countries; and the consequences of possible armed conflicts—as is now the case in the Ukraine—and natural disasters, caused, in large part, by human pollution. Moreover, the word "revolution" used to qualify some of these factors is applied in its entire meaning: the overthrow of long-established systems in favour of new ways of thinking and doing things. Each country must adopt the necessary measures to adapt to this new concept of globalization which is both more realistic and more unified.

Towards Increased International Solidarity

Thus, the new cycle of globalization that is currently underway could also involve a major shift towards a greater international solidarity, given the impact of these changes within the context of the strong interdependencies that will be created by these new bilateral and regional free trade agreements, for which negotiations are in progress or soon to be started.

The most problematic aspect of this close interdependence remains the harmful economic consequences that a state's poor governance could have on its partners by triggering a domino effect such as we saw during the 2008 crisis. The positive aspect is that governments will be required to increase vigilance and foster solidarity, thus complementing the globalization process on a geopolitical level as well as an economic one. This is evidenced by the situation in the Ukraine, where Russia's violation of international law did not initially draw gunfire from other countries but instead hard-hitting economic sanctions.

Thus, a new international order could result from this close relationship between states, insofar as we are able to adapt our international organizations to it. The integrity of borders and respect for the sovereignty of states must remain at the heart of international law; however, they must be interpreted within the framework of a more intelligent, more universal globalization.

The general conclusion of this book is therefore that the global economy should bring us into a new era of prosperity, as long as we make the right decisions going forward. As Angel Gurría, Secretary-General of the OECD, stated in his introduction to this book, the 2008 crisis confirmed that continuing along the same path would be a grave error and provided us with an opportunity to rethink our economic policies. We must, however, adjust to a more modest growth rate than we were used to prior to 2008. Technological advancement should compensate for this lack of economic growth to some degree by contributing more and more to quality of life, as it will lead to a reorganization of work and resulting social changes.

Emerging nations must prepare themselves for a period of near-stagnation, in some cases, and face the threat of deflation in others. The emerging countries will have the difficult task of sustaining their domestic market growth and encouraging the emergence of a middle class that has already adopted new consumer habits, while controlling inflation. Here too, technological advancements should help these countries shift away from a convergence with the West which, with its current dynamic of dependence, is becoming increasingly obsolete.

While the latest statistics from the WTO show that international trade increased by just 2.3% in 2012, world trade remains the cornerstone of this new growth era that is emerging from this new economic cycle. It seems safe to say that, at first, the multilateral aspect will have less of a role to play than it did during the first globalization cycle, which began with the creation of the WTO in 1994. Meanwhile, the WTO ministerial conference held in Bali in December 2013 has given us reason to hope that we can breathe new life into the Doha Round and thus into globalization itself. Multilateralism must now include, in a complementary manner, bilateralism and regionalism with regard to the major issues that we are facing. Intellectual property, in particular, comes to mind as it must support technological advancement, which will change our lives in the coming years, and agriculture, which must enable us to feed the planet without destroying it in the process.

In light of the above, the slow and hesitant pace at which the economy is recovering is not entirely negative. We need to take advantage of the opportunity that is provided to carefully implement the changes that will give this new growth era at our door the building blocks required to ensure its sustainability and compatibility with the newly defined notions of democracy, liberty and equity that we want to give to humanity.

GIL RÉMILLARD

HISTORY AND MISSION

THE CONFERENCE OF MONTREAL

The International Economic Forum of the Americas—Conference of Montreal was first held in 1995, as the economic globalization movement was gaining momentum with the creation of the World Trade Organization (WTO) and the North American Free Trade Agreement (NAFTA). At that time, questions were being raised about the real consequences that this new worldwide economic integration could have on both industrialized countries and "emerging countries"—as they became known a few years later.

The International Economic Forum of the Americas—Conference of Montreal has the following mission:

To heighten knowledge and awareness of the major issues concerning economic globalization, with a particular emphasis on the relations between the Americas and other continents. The Conference also strives to foster information sharing and to promote free discussion on major current economic issues. His mission is also to facilitate meetings between world leaders and to encourage international discourse by bringing together heads of state, business people, members of the government, international leaders, academics, members of workers associations and members of civil society.

The objectives of the conference are:

- To develop knowledge on the major challenges faced by the Americas in the global economy;
- To give its participants access to privileged information while fostering free and extensive discussions on various aspects of

economy with contributors and experts from among the best qualified worldwide;

- To promote relations between governments, international organizations, business people, members of civil society, workers associations and universities
- To allow its participants from various areas in the world to have business meetings during which they can develop their company or organization internationally
- To cultivate a better understanding of major international issues in order to make international economic development more equitable and sensitive to specific realities in designated areas of the world

Other activities:

The International Economic Forum of the Americas also hosts:

- The Toronto Global Forum, held each year in October;
- The World Strategic Forum, held each year in April in Miami.

MIX
Paper from
responsible sources
FSC® C103567
FSC
www.fsc.org